Also by Charles W. Whalen, Jr.

How to End the Draft: The Case for an
All-Volunteer Army (with Frank J. Horton,
Richard S. Schweiker, Garner E. Shriver
and Robert T. Stafford)

YOUR RIGHT TO KNOW

YOUR RIGHT TO KNOW

CHARLES W. WHALEN, JR.

Vintage Books

A Division of Random House
New York

VINTAGE BOOKS EDITION APRIL 1973

Copyright © 1973 by Charles W. Whalen, Jr.

Library of Congress Catalog
Card Number: 73-4390
ISBN: 0-394-71957-3

Manufactured in the United States of America

CONTENTS

INTRODUCTION

We are a people of superlatives. Perhaps that is because we inhabit a country in which everything is so much bigger than the countries from which most of our ancestors came. We think of our land itself as the biggest, the wealthiest, in its variety the prettiest. The hyperstatement is thus a way of life with us.

And so each generation of journalists has been inclined to believe that the attacks against the press in its own time are the worst ever and that the threats to the freedom of press and speech are the most dangerous ever.

Indeed, there have been some rough periods—very rough. Right after the nation's founding, the principle of a free press was tested with the Alien and Sedition Acts of 1798 that would have jailed anyone who wrote or spoke with "intent to defame" the government. That law lasted only two and a half years and helped bring down President Adams' Federalist Party, but it shook the timbers of press freedom while it lasted.

That was the start. As late as the forties and fifties of this century there were recurring suggestions that journalists be licensed. There were Congressional demands for investigations of newspaper bias following the 1952 election (television had not yet come into its own as the *bête noire* of parties in power).

But even with this perspective on the past, it is possible for a journalist of *this* generation to state with deep conviction that the crisis today may really be the worst ever.

The reasons are several. For one thing, there is the attitude of President Nixon's Administration. It probably finds press criticism no less distasteful than administrations that preceded it, but the unprecedented difference is the organized, concerted nature of its attack on the press, as Congressman Whalen points out in his preface to this book.

This, in turn, as probably planned, tended to politicize the issue of a free press. To be for press freedom was to be against the Nixon Administration. An atmosphere has been created wherein a large body of our citizens, perhaps even a majority, is inclined to dismiss the alarm with which the press views its condition as just some more liberal, leftist, elitist, Eastern-establishment anti-Nixon propaganda, although the readers of such conservative newspapers as the *Chicago Tribune* and the *Indianapolis News* and many others must be confused by their editors' equally strong concern.

The truth is so apparent to a working journalist that it beggars his understanding as to why others cannot see. Why can't the American people see that freedom of the press is not some privilege extended to a favored segment of the population but is purely and simply their own right to be told what their government and its servants are doing in their name?

The atmosphere the Administration created exploded in the Supreme Court's so-called Caldwell decision of June 29, 1972. It stripped journalists of one of their principal working tools—the right to talk to news sources in confidence and to protect those sources.

The judges and the attorneys, the justices and the constitutional experts can argue this matter until they are blue in the face. The fact is that there are few working journalists who believe that freedom of the press and, hence, democracy can endure with newsmen so hobbled.

There are bills now before Congress that would recognize the confidentiality of news sources: so-called shield laws to protect the press from harassment by subpoena. Congressman Whalen is the sponsor of one of them. It happens that I do not agree with the conditions his bill would impose on newsmen's privilege. I think that conditions are loopholes and that newsmen's privilege of confidentiality must be absolute except only in cases of libel.

But this is getting into the very substance of the book to follow. What should be said here is that even as Mr. Whalen himself points out, it is not important that all of us agree on every aspect of a shield law—the details can be worked out. It is important beyond all measure, however, that the citizenry understand the history of the conflict, the terms of the engagement, and the shadow that its outcome will cast on the American future.

This book contributes a major source to that understanding.

Walter Cronkite

February 14, 1973

PREFACE

Two years ago, as I intensified my efforts to obtain additional co-sponsors for the Newsmen's Privilege Act, I expanded my search for supportive material. After all, the issue of the so-called shield for journalists was relatively obscure. Along with most other persons, therefore, my knowledge of the subject—its historical antecedents and its legal precedents—was extremely limited.

In the course of gathering data, I was helped in many instances by the Library of Congress and journalism scholars. But it soon became clear that there was no one compendium detailing the history, legal and journalistic, of the newsman's right to maintain the confidentiality of his sources and information.

As the incidence of newsmen's subpoenas accelerated during the following months, I broadened my study in preparation for the Congressional debate that seemed inevitable. Then, as my role in the newsmen's privilege issue became more prominent, I began to receive numerous inquiries from interested students and legislators who, like me, could find no single reference source. Thus was born the idea for this undertaking.

In synthesizing my files and data in book form, my purpose is threefold.

First, it is my hope that the general reader will be alerted to the dangers to his "right to know" which are inherent in the subpoenaing of reporters.

Second, the book is intended to aid those interested in studying the newsmen's "shield" question in greater depth.

Journalism and law students may find it helpful in comprehending the realities working reporters have had to face since *New York Times* reporter James Simonton was confronted with the subpoena dilemma in 1857.

Third, I trust that this book will contribute to the legislative dialogue that will take place this year in the Congress and in numerous state assemblies.

Many people deserve my sincerest thanks for their contributions to the publication of this book. William D. Wick rates a special commendation. His background in journalism and American history at Northwestern University, and his current study at the Georgetown University Law Center, uniquely qualified him for his research and editing roles. My executive assistant, William P. Steponkus, provided me with continuing motivation in seeing the project through to its completion. Ms. Patricia A. Mooney, my legislative assistant, made many valuable suggestions which enhanced the documentation of the issue. To the helpful women, Mrs. Mattie Mernone, Mrs. Doris Post and Mrs. Ginnie Ashford, who put the words in readable form on paper, goes my deepest appreciation. And I am very grateful to Anne Freedgood, of Random House, for her constructive assistance and her willingness to undertake publication of this book.

Charles W. Whalen, Jr.
Member of Congress

February 1, 1973
Washington, D.C.

PART I

THE PROBLEM IN CONTEXT

1

The American Press under Siege

Attacks on press freedom throughout the world increased in 1972. The International Press Institute warned in its annual report that "the true danger lies in the fact that a growing number of governments, parliamentary representatives, citizens and even some members of the press begin to accept that attacks on freedom of expression are legitimate and justifiable."[1]

The IPI, which has seventeen hundred members in sixty-two non-Communist countries, singled out Japan as the one major exception to the generally gloomy review. "The Japanese press," said the report, "is free, powerful and conscious of its responsibilities in the life of society."[2]

It was a sobering report. As the *Chicago Tribune* said of it, "what is most distressing—though not surprising—is that for the first time it had harsh words for the United States, which was founded with the cry to 'let freedom ring' and which has hitherto served the world as a model of freedom."[3] The report observed that in the United States the government "in various guises is attempting to chip away at press freedom through the courts and by threats of court action."[4]

The American press has been under siege during the past four years. If a beginning to the series of confrontations between the government and the media must be assigned, it undoubtedly would be November 1969, when Vice-President Spiro T. Agnew criticized the television networks. Wittingly or otherwise, the Vice-President served to initiate a period in which journalists clearly considered themselves threatened by the federal government as never before in our history. As an American citizen, Agnew had the right to speak his mind about the networks; as a public official, he had the right and often the responsibility to speak out on issues of importance. However, the crucial factor in the Des Moines speech was Agnew's articulation of the relationship between the Vice-President and the television networks. He reminded the networks of the fact that they existed under "a monopoly sanctioned and licensed by government."[5]

Although the Vice-President repeatedly denied that he was threatening the networks, the fact that he spoke as the second highest official in the government—the government that had the power to "sanction and license" the networks —generated substantial alarm. As CBS President Frank Stanton stated, "It is far more shocking to me that the utterances of the second-ranking official of the United States government require such repeated assurances that he had in mind no violation of the Constitution than it is comforting to have them at all."[6]

The Vice-President's intentions might have been ambiguous; the effects of his remarks were not. A few weeks later, when President Nixon delivered another speech on Vietnam, the "network analysis" that the Vice-President had criticized had been eliminated. As *TV Guide* observed:

> Vice President Spiro T. Agnew's scolding of the networks apparently had the desired result: after President Nixon's December 8 press conference, there was no criticism whatever from the commentators who followed him.[7]

In September 1970 the Vice-President criticized the playing of songs on radio that related to "drug culture propaganda." In March 1971 the Federal Communications Commission issued a ruling requiring broadcasters not to air songs that "would promote or glorify the use of illegal drugs." Further, stations were warned that they could lose their licenses if they did not adhere to the ruling.[8]

Similar attacks on other aspects of the broadcast media followed, and in December 1972 further escalation occurred. Dr. Clay Whitehead, director of the White House Office of Telecommunications Policy, criticized the content of network news programs. He made it clear that the administration wanted local broadcast affiliates to weed out the alleged bias. Whitehead said that "station managers and network officials who fail to act to correct imbalance or consistent bias in the network—or who acquiesce by silence—can only be considered willing participants, to be held fully accountable at license renewal time."[9]

A legislative package embodying Whitehead's proposals is expected to be presented to the Congress (although speculation developed that his remarks may have been a "trial balloon" with modifications to ensue). As the *Washington Post* noted, the legislation "will come complete with incentives for docile local affiliates." The *Post* continued:

Along with new responsibility, they would get a couple of breaks they have long wanted: First, the license period will be expanded from three to five years; and second, challenges either by community groups or by a hopeful alternative applicant for the license are to be made more difficult. It is a neat horse trade. The local station owners would be given warm and gentle treatment in exchange for the requirement that they scrutinize the network's news offerings for "bias." At the same time, Dr. Whitehead's colorful language gives them a pretty good clue as to what kind of "bias" the government will expect them to have eliminated by license renewal time.[10]

The battle that electronic journalists must wage to attempt to report independently is already difficult, and it may soon be insurmountable.

"Unless there is a drastic change in the atmosphere already generated by the Nixon administration in its first four years," said *Washington Post* television commentator Alan Kriegsman, "we appear to be headed for an era of timidity, fecklessness and bland program content, on both commercial and public TV."[11]

Freedom and independence have not been secure for the print media either.

In June 1971 the Justice Department sought to enjoin publication by the *New York Times* and *Washington Post* of the Pentagon Papers, a detailed intragovernmental history of the U.S. involvement in the Vietnam war. It was the first time since the adoption of the Bill of Rights that the government asked that federal courts halt publication. And the government did shut down the presses on the story for fourteen days before the Supreme Court ruled that the material could be printed. Although the newspapers "won," they nevertheless were restrained from publishing for two weeks, and the opinions in the case left cause for future concern.

The intensified assault on press freedoms threatens us all. Journalistic freedom and independence must be strengthened. That is not to say that the press is above criticism. In fact, vigorous criticism of American journalism is healthy for both the press and the nation, and criticism is often richly deserved. But many of today's attacks transcend the bounds of mere critical comment.

The climate today is such that the president of the Cleveland Fraternal Order of Police could seriously suggest that the government should license newspapers to ensure accuracy in the media.[12]

In September–October 1971 and February 1972 Senator Sam Ervin (D–N.C.), chairman of the Senate Subcommittee on Constitutional Rights, held hearings on the freedom of the press in America. He indicated that the hearings were scheduled "because it is apparent that in today's America, many people doubt the vitality and significance of the first amendment's guarantee of freedom of the press."[13]

The First Amendment to the United States Constitution —part of the Bill of Rights—was demanded by the citizens as protection against government encroachment upon a free press. There was no guarantee of freedom of speech, press or assembly in the original draft of the Constitution of the United States. Charles Pinckney, a delegate to the Constitutional Convention from South Carolina, attempted to insert a clause to specify such freedoms, but his recommendation was rejected. Most delegates felt it was unnecessary since the powers of Congress did not extend to the press. Alexander Hamilton, for instance, supported the omission, believing that the people and the government naturally would protect such freedoms without their having to be guaranteed.[14]

But the American public of the late 1780s was not pleased with the omission.[15] The absence of written protection of the rights of speech, press and assembly aroused anger and condemnation at state conventions. The popular desire for an enumeration of rights and liberties in the new Constitution was so great that a "Bill of Rights"—ten amendments to the original document—was ratified on December 15, 1791. The first of those ten amendments, vital and eloquent in its simplicity, has been familiar to virtually all Americans since 1791:

> Congress shall make no law respecting an establishment of religion, or prohibiting the free exercise thereof; or abridging the freedom of speech, or of the press; or the right of the people peaceably to assemble, and to petition the Government for a redress of grievances.[16]

Thus, from the very beginning in this country, there has been a special recognition accorded to the importance of freedom of speech and freedom of the press.

As Thomas Jefferson once observed:

> The way to prevent these irregular interpositions of the people is to give them full information of their affairs through the channels of the public papers, and to contrive that those papers should penetrate the whole mass of the people. The basis of our government being the opinion of the people, the very first object should be to keep that right; and were it left to me to decide whether we should have a government without newspapers, or newspapers without a government, I should not hesitate a moment to prefer the latter.[17]

Rhetoric on the importance of a free press has continued for nearly two hundred years, but First Amendment values still do not occupy the position they should in our society. With all of the glowing phrases spoken about the First Amendment and the respect Americans ostensibly accord to the concepts embodied therein, the freedoms it guarantees have come under constant attack—and by decent, law-abiding citizens as well as by government officials.

Today more than ever before there is a divergence between our words and our actions relating to freedom of speech and freedom of the press. A portion of an opinion authored almost two decades ago by Pennsylvania Supreme Court Justice Michael Musmanno is illustrative:

> That we should have to argue at this high hour in the day of civilization in behalf of the rights of the press to speak and act unrestrictedly in obtaining and reporting news is astonishing. After all the decisions which have been rendered, the books which have been written, the crusades which have been waged, the sermons which have been preached, and the lectures which have been delivered on freedom of the press; after witnessing every day, almost every hour, that freedom of the press is a living, breathing thing, constantly blossoming on the tree of tangible demonstration, it seems like defending the North Star to descant at length on the need of a free press in a free democracy. And yet, it appears that from time to time the most obvious truism is attacked and the most commonplace virtue is derided, and, as a consequence, one finds oneself defending the integrity of the multiplication table, the sanctity of mother love, and the need of milk in growing children.[18]

The hearings conducted by Senator Ervin bore witness to the fact that the dynamic, independent press envisioned by the First Amendment and extolled by Jefferson is in jeopardy. We appear to be living in a time when "the most obvious truism is attacked and the most commonplace virtue is derided."

One of the principal issues considered during the hearings was the use of the subpoena by the government to

compel reporters to divulge confidential sources and information. Senator Ervin briefly outlined the problem on the
first day of hearings:

> In recent years an increasing number of subpoenas have
> been issued to newsmen in connection with various Gov-
> ernment investigations. In the past, government prosecu-
> tors and members of the press have attempted to adjust
> their different interests in a way that would serve justice
> without endangering freedom of the press. Apparently,
> the mutual understanding on the part of the press and
> the Government which underlay this adjustment of in-
> terest has disappeared, perhaps another victim of the fear
> and suspicion that has developed between them. Con-
> frontation has replaced negotiation. Today, there are
> members of the press who believe that their integrity and
> independence is being threatened by Government's zeal-
> ous demand for their notes, their pictures, their films,
> and other working materials. Senator James Pearson of
> Kansas and Congressman Charles Whalen of Ohio, have
> introduced legislation in the Senate and House of Repre-
> sentatives to establish a statutory privilege for newsmen to
> protect their confidential information and sources from
> compulsory disclosure.[19]

The problem of reporters being forced to reveal their
confidential sources and information to government authorities is crucial if we are to benefit from a truly free
press. And this disturbing development becomes even more
ominous when placed in the context of the previously cited
infringements on the independence of the press.

As the law stands today (except in the nineteen states
which have enacted specific statutes to protect reporters), a
journalist is not legally entitled to withhold confidential
sources and information if the government requests them.
Thus, to comply with the law, a reporter must violate the
Code of Ethics adopted by the American Newspaper Guild

in 1934, which declares that "newspapermen shall refuse to reveal confidences or disclose sources of confidential information in court or before other judicial or investigative bodies."[20]

Most important, however, is the effect that the power to subpoena has on the flow of news to the American public. As will be demonstrated in succeeding chapters, if the law continues to grant government the power to use the subpoena to harass, intimidate, or secure information from journalists, the independence and news-gathering ability of the press is significantly impaired.

Numerous other countries already provide reporters with protection against compelled testimony. Sweden enables journalists to protect the identity of confidential sources except for a stated category of documents where the identity of the source is vital to the case.[21] In Finland reporters do not have to reveal sources unless there are important reasons—such as a major crime or national security—involved in a case.[22] Most of the states in the Federal Republic of Germany extend a broad testimonial privilege to reporters.[23] Austria also provides protection.[24]

In America, a country historically regarded as a champion of freedom of the press, there is no such protection. The proposition advanced in this book is that American journalists should be protected by a "privilege" not to testify.

Legislation to protect reporters from forced disclosure of information has often been referred to as a "newsmen's privilege act." Although the legal terminology is correct, the label is misleading. The purpose of such protection is not to confer a special benefit on journalists but rather to assure the unimpeded flow of news to the American public. Therefore, a more accurate title—and the one used for the legislation I have introduced in the Ninety-third Congress —is the Free Flow of Information Act.

The succeeding chapters provide a history of the "privilege" cases in America, an examination of the landmark case of *Branzburg v. Hayes*,[25] a look at the most recent cases and the arguments for and against the privilege.

The earliest case of conflict between the government and the press occurred four decades before the American revolution with the trial of John Peter Zenger, the printer, publisher and editor of the *New York Weekly Journal*. In 1734 the *Journal* published a number of articles that were critical of the governor of New York, William Cosby. Governor Cosby had provoked considerable controversy by prosecuting the interim governor and by removing the chief justice from office.

Zenger was arrested on November 17, 1734, charged with criminal libel. He was unable to post bond and waited nine months in jail before his trial on August 4, 1735. Zenger was represented by Andrew Hamilton after Governor Cosby disbarred Zenger's original lawyer. Hamilton was one of the most distinguished trial lawyers in the colonies, and he made a moving appeal to the jury to acquit Zenger of the libel charge. The verdict was "Not guilty," and the case has long been considered a landmark for freedom of the press.

The concept of a testimonial privilege was not at issue during the trial, and thus no ruling was made on a reporter's right to shield confidential sources or information. However, throughout his imprisonment and the trial, Zenger did not reveal the names of the individuals who wrote articles for the *Journal*, even though the governor had offered a reward of fifty pounds for the identity of the author of the allegedly libelous articles. Thus Zenger's silence did serve to establish as a part of a journalist's "code of ethics" a prohibition against revealing sources of information. Other printers had similar confrontations with the government during the eighteenth century as angry officials demanded to know who wrote critical articles.

Press/government conflicts continued in the nineteenth century. In 1812, for example, an *Alexandria Herald* reporter, Nathaniel Rounsavelt, refused to tell the House of Representatives his sources for an article about secret House action on an embargo. The earliest major recorded case which brought the issue sharply into focus, however, occurred in 1857. It was the first in a series of cases, which will be examined next, in which the legislative branch of government tried to pry information from reporters.

PART II

THE CASES

2

The Conflict
in the
Legislative Arena

We know that a corrupt organization of Members of
Congress and certain lobby agents at Washington has
existed since early in the session last year. We are well
satisfied that this organization holds the balance of power
in its hands sufficient, in most cases, to kill or carry
any measure pending in the House of Representatives,
and that its power has been exerted in favor of measures
where its price ($1,000 per vote generally, or its equiva-
lent) was agreed to; and that it has been used to prevent
favorable action on equally meritorious measures which
were unable or unwilling to submit to the piratical
tribute.

This organization is confined to no party, but embraces
members of them all—for it is a singular and notorious
fact, that while patriotism can rise above partisan con-

siderations, villainy can. There are many of those connected with it, we do not doubt, who have been brought into it by the devices of others, and without any full conviction on their own minds of its real character. But of its existence, and its power over legislation, there can be as little doubt as there is of its turpitude, and of the duty of the public press to expose it to the knowledge and condemnation of the country.[1]

So *The New York Times* editorialized on January 6, 1857. Reporter James Simonton had revealed through a series of articles that Congressmen were taking bribes in exchange for their votes on certain measures, and the *Times* did not permit the issue to rest. In fact, the *Times*' articles and editorials caused such a furor in the House of Representatives that a five-member select committee was appointed by the Speaker to investigate the charges.

Even before the investigation was initiated, however, the charges were substantiated in part. Representative Robert Paine (American–N.C.), admitting he knew "nothing about the editor of that journal [*The Times*] or of the journal itself," independently confirmed the substance of Simonton's stories:

> I say now distinctly upon this floor, that there is not an entire want of truth in the allegations contained in that article; that a distinct proposition has been made by a Member of this House, and in regard to the Minnesota land bill, that $1,500 would be guaranteed to a Member for his vote for that bill . . .[2]

The select committee summoned Simonton on January 15, 1857, and asked him to reveal the sources of information for his articles. He refused, saying, "I cannot without a violation of confidence, than which I would rather suffer anything."[3] The committee released the reporter, giving

him "time for reflection on the consequences of his refusal."
He was recalled by the committee five days later and was
again asked to divulge his sources. Again he refused:

> The result of my deliberation upon the subject has been
> to confirm me in the opinion that, whatever penalty
> I may suffer, I cannot answer that question. I beg the
> committee to understand that I have no other motive
> whatever in declining but the simple one I have stated
> before—that I do not see how I can answer it without a
> dishonorable breach of confidence.[4]

The committee did not understand. It recommended that
the House vote to command the sergeant at arms to take
Simonton into custody. The select committee chairman,
Representative James Orr (D–S.C.), argued against any
leniency for Simonton:

> If a man feels that there is so much of personal deg-
> radation that he cannot violate confidence even to pro-
> tect the supremacy of the law, let the consequences of
> that sublimated virtue which he may be supposed to
> possess be visited, and visited properly and severely,
> upon him.[5]

Other Congressmen were quick to concur with Orr.
Representative Henry Davis (American–Md.) denigrated
the "perverse principle of honor" that prevented Simonton
from making the requested disclosure.[6] Representative
Hiram Warner (D–Ga.) contended that Simonton was
bound by duty to answer the questions "no matter how
sacred the confidence which may have been reposed in
him."[7]

No one defended the concept of a legal privilege for
reporters. Several House members were opposed to the
committee's recommendation, but their opposition was not

based on their support for Simonton's position. Representative Henry Burnett (D–Ky.), the strongest opponent of the recommendation, felt that the House lacked the authority to punish Simonton, but that the reporter nevertheless "richly merits punishment."[8]

Simonton was permitted to address the House. Although he did not have prepared remarks, he eloquently defended his position as a journalist and the reasons for his silence:

> I am no speaker; I am no lawyer; I am a member of the press; and though unaccustomed to address public bodies or meetings, I stand here with a firm reliance on the correctness of the position I have taken, and a full conviction that I am pursuing the path of duty . . .
>
> . . . gentlemen came to me and bound me to secrecy. I accorded the confidence unreservedly, not knowing what they had to communicate—whether an important public document—important to my readers; whether it was an important fact to control or affect my own judgment in regard to the discharge of my duties, or whatever it might be. I had the right, I maintain, to receive their confidence for my own purposes . . .
>
> What I have done is this: Having been convinced that corruption did exist—having a moral conviction of that fact—and I venture to assert that scarcely a gentleman upon this floor is without the same moral conviction—having this moral conviction, I felt it, as a member of the press, my right and duty to denounce it upon such moral conviction. Sir, it is a matter more than of right; it is a question of duty. You have a responsibility to your constituency; I, as a member of the press, have mine to a constituency.[9]

Simonton's speech did not alter the intentions of the House. On January 21, 1857, the House voted 136–23 to hold Simonton in contempt, and placed him in custody of the sergeant at arms.

Nineteen days later, however, the committee recommended Simonton's discharge; the committee had become convinced that the reporter would never reveal his sources. The House adopted the committee's recommendations, and Simonton was released.

In addition, the select committee determined that Simonton's charges were true—without learning his sources. In fact, the committee recommended the expulsion of three House members, who thereupon resigned. During the next two decades more than a dozen similar conflicts occurred.

In 1870, for instance, the *New York Evening Post* published an article indicating that Cuban leaders had spent large sums of money in attempts to influence Congressional votes on the recognition of the Cuban republic. The story stated that it was not known who accepted bribes but that payments definitely had been offered. It appeared in the June 6, 1870, edition of the *Post*. The reporter who wrote the article, W. Scott Smith, based his account on documents he received from a confidential source.

In June 1870 Smith acceded to a request to testify before the House of Representatives. He was asked to identify the person who gave him the documents. "I would say that the documents were shown to me confidentially," said Smith, "and that it would be a violation of good faith to make public the source from which these documents were obtained."[10]

A resolution then was introduced to expel Smith from the reporters' gallery. A select committee was also appointed to examine the charges against Smith ("having slandered a member of the House, and having declined to give the source of the information upon which he alleges he based his statement").

The committee, after studying the matter, recommended that Smith *not* be expelled:

> While the committee considers that the correspondent of the *Evening Post* has not been without fault, they are

also of the opinion that his fault is not of such flagrant character as to justify his expulsion from the gallery, or even to warrant any formal resolution of censure.[11]

Only one year after the Smith incident, the *New York Tribune* published what the newspaper alleged to be a copy of the Treaty of Washington—an agreement under consideration at that time by the Senate. The treaty appeared in the May 11, 1871, issue.

Since the matter was being scrutinized by the Senate in executive session, it was officially classified secret. However, the Secretary of State had published a summary of the contents before the *Tribune* printed it. Further, a number of government officials, including the President, were in favor of releasing the entire text of the treaty. Thus, no damaging "national secrets" were made public. As Senator Allen Thurman (D–Ohio) noted at the time: "It will not do to say that there has been a heinous offense or any moral guilt in the publication that has been made."[12]

Nevertheless, the Senate was disturbed by the publication of the treaty. A select committee was appointed the day following the printing of the newspaper story to investigate the matter. *Tribune* reporters Zeb White and Hiram Ramsdell were subpoenaed by the committee. They admitted that they had dispatched the contents of the treaty to the *Tribune*, but they refused to tell the committee the source of their information.

White and Ramsdell were released and then recalled. Again they were questioned about their sources for the article about the treaty. Again they refused:

White: I respectfully refuse to answer.
The Chairman: Why do you refuse to answer the question?
White: On account of my professional honor.

The Chairman: Not because you are unable to answer?

White: No, sir.

The Chairman: What do you mean by your professional honor?

White: Whenever I receive any item of news, unless I have the permission of the gentleman or person who furnishes to me that item of news, I consider it as an honorable thing that I shall not divulge the source of that news.[13]

Several days later the Senate committed them into the custody of the sergeant at arms.

The *Tribune*, in the meantime, made it clear that its support of the two reporters was unequivocal. The newspaper publicly stated that White and Ramsdell would receive double their normal salaries as long as they were imprisoned.[14]

Senators continued to defend the contempt findings on the basis of the supremacy of the law. Senator Matthew Carpenter (R–Wis.) expressed the view of most of his colleagues:

The pretense upon which the witness refused to answer the questions put to him by the committee is that, being a correspondent of a public newspaper, and having received a communication in confidence, he is not at liberty to disclose it. The consequence of this proposition is that the privilege of a newspaper correspondent overrides the Constitution of the United States and the acts of Congress passed in pursuance thereof, which by the Constitution itself are declared to be the supreme law of the land.[15]

And the *Tribune* vigorously justified its actions in publishing the treaty and in concealing the names of the sources for it:

The Senate may well learn one thing, without further
making itself ridiculous by impotent fault-finding about
a publication which the whole country approves. It is not
our business to keep the secrets of the government, but to
publish the news. If the government can't keep its own
secrets, we do not propose to undertake for it the contract. There does not live in Washington the officer, high
or low, who can honestly say the *Tribune* ever received
from him in confidence any document, or verbal or
written statement of any sort, which it betrayed; and no
man better knows this fact than the head of the Department most affected by our publication of the Treaty of
Washington. But when news comes to us, and no public
interest seems to us imperiled, we print it.[16]

The Senate debate ultimately centered on the issue of
whether that body possessed the power to imprison the
reporters beyond the end of the legislative session. Because
of doubts about such power, White and Ramsdell were
released when the Senate adjourned, and the incident
ended.

Newspaper articles charging bribery in Washington offi-
cialdom appeared again in 1894. This time it was alleged
that senators had taken bribes from sugar-trust lobbyists in
exchange for votes for beneficial amendments to the Wil-
son-Gorman tariff bill.

The Senate established a select committee which subpoenaed two reporters—Elisha Edwards of the *Philadelphia Press* and John Shriver of the *New York Mail and
Express*. Both refused to disclose the sources of the information that led to their stories about corrupt Senate
practices.

The two reporters were certified to the District of Columbia district attorney and an indictment against them was
returned by a grand jury. The District of Columbia Supreme Court required the defendants to enter a plea. The
decision left no doubt about the court's views on the issue:

Let it once be established that the editor or correspondent cannot be called upon in any proceeding to disclose the information upon which the publication in his journals are based, and the great barrier against libelous publication is at once stricken down, and the greatest possible temptation created to use the public press as a means of disseminating scandal, thereby tending to lessen, if not destroy its power and usefulness.[17]

Journalists had lost again.

Three years later another bribery charge was printed—this time on the West Coast. The *San Francisco Examiner* in 1897 accused California state senators of the impropriety. A news editor and a reporter for the *Examiner* were brought before the state senate. A.M. Lawrence and L.L. Levings were interrogated about their sources for the articles but would not reveal them.

The California Senate voted to punish the men for contempt. But Lawrence and Levings obtained a writ of habeas corpus and appealed to the Supreme Court of California. The court discharged the writ, thereby affirming the contempt conviction: "It cannot be successfully contended, and has not been seriously argued, that the witnesses were justified in refusing to give the names upon the grounds that the communications were privileged."[18]

Another state legislature became embroiled in a privilege controversy in 1934—and this one began with a letter to the editor. The *Louisville Courier-Journal* published a communication titled "The Psalm of Politics" in its "Point of View" letters column in March 1934. The contents were very critical of alleged corruption in the state legislature as the following excerpts indicate:

Whose government is it? It doesn't belong to the people any more. Oh, yes, they elected representatives and senators to come here and make laws, tear up laws, tax every darn thing imaginable, give every other person in the state of Kentucky a job, but when they come here, they do as they darn please—that is enough of them that have a machine behind them saying, "Go on. Go on. Don't you see it's a chance to make some money out of it for ourselves? Why there will be 50 jobs for us to give away."

Let the bill speak for itself:

"The floor leader is my shepherd. I shall not want (unless it pleases him). He maketh me lie down in the committees; he leadeth me to a watery grave; he leadeth me into the paths of wrongness for Kentucky's sake; he restoreth my soul (if 51 members want it); Yea, though I walk through the valley of the shadow of death, I shall fear no evil, for the Speaker, thou art with me; the administration and the Governor, they comfort me. Thou preparest to table me in the presence of other factions, thou annointest my head with amendments; my cup is turned over. Surely politics and corruption shall follow me all the days of my life, and I shall dwell in the house of the politician forever."[19]

The letter was signed: "A Member of the House of Representatives." A committee of the Kentucky House of Representatives ordered L. Vance Armentrout, acting editor of the *Courier-Journal*, to testify and furnish the name of their colleague who wrote the letter. Armentrout said he was unable to do so because it would violate the confidence imposed on him by the writer. Armentrout was jailed but obtained his release one hour later on a writ of habeas corpus. Finally, by a vote of sixty-five to twenty, he was fined twenty-five dollars by the Kentucky House of Representatives.

The next major controversy between the government and the press concerning forced testimony occurred in 1943 during World War II. The *Akron Beacon-Journal* ran a piece which contended that because of union rules, member seamen would not unload vital military cargo on Guadalcanal on a Sunday. The *Beacon-Journal* allegations were published in newspapers throughout the nation. The Committee on Naval Affairs of the U.S. House of Representatives quickly called city editor Charles C. Miller to Washington.

Miller, asked to identify the marines who gave him the information, refused to do so. The committee did *not* seek to punish Miller by bringing contempt charges against him. In fact, the committee tacitly recognized the right of a journalist to withhold confidential information:

> It would have been helpful had the paper seen fit to submit to us these names, which we assured the publisher would be kept in confidence so as to minimize the possibility of military recrimination. We are aware, however, of the customary practice of newspapers in not revealing the sources of such stories.[20]

In 1945 another House committee began an investigation in the aftermath of articles published by a periodical. *PM* magazine reporter Albert Deutsch had written a series containing criticism of medical programs for veterans. In May 1945 the House Veterans Committee asked Deutsch to divulge the names of the Veterans Administration authorities who had given him information for the articles. Deutsch said that his professional ethics did not permit him to answer the question. The committee initially cited Deutsch for contempt, but eleven days after the original vote it reversed itself. By a vote of thirteen to two, the charges against Deutsch were dropped.

In early 1952 Edward Milne, the Washington correspondent for the *Providence Journal and Bulletin*, reported that the Senate Subcommittee on Privileges and Elections recommended in an unpublished report that hearings on charges against Senator Joseph McCarthy (R–Wis.) should proceed. In a second story a month later, Milne revealed that the staff investigation had included an examination of McCarthy's personal finances and income-tax records.

After the publication of the second story, Milne was subpoenaed by the subcommittee and instructed to produce all documents, notes, memoranda and other papers relating to the origin and publication of the two stories. Milne appeared before the subcommittee in April 1952 and offered the following statement:

> With all due respect to the members of the subcommittee, I am unable to disclose my sources of information on the stories in question, for the following reasons:
>
> (1) I gave my promise to my sources that under no circumstances would I make them known. To break that promise would be a dishonorable act.
>
> (2) To disclose my sources would, in effect, be to bring my newspaper career to a close. No reporter can last in the newspaper business who violates a confidence. Neither my own newspaper nor any other would have any use for my services if I disclosed my sources on these stories. And I would be an object of well-deserved contempt among my colleagues if I violated the confidence placed in me by my sources.[21]

Milne was given until May 12, 1952, to adhere to the subpoena. On May 7, however, Senator Guy Gillette (D–Iowa) announced that the subpoena was being withdrawn. Although the senator did not pursue the issue, he indicated that he felt he *could* have. He said that the Senate could have cited Milne for contempt but that there "had been recognition that in the public welfare . . . too close an inquiry shall not be made into sources of information" of reporters.[22]

Again in 1963, committees in the House and Senate were reluctant to become involved in a battle with the press over the privilege issue. Washington journalist Jack Anderson authored a *Parade* magazine article in 1963 concerning Congressmen who allegedly "cheated" by padding payrolls, selling influence and misusing public funds. The House Administration Committee asked Anderson to reveal the names of his informants but he refused. Anderson asserted a privilege, claiming that reporters possessed a Constitutional right to protect their sources of information. The Committee chairman, Congressman Omar Burleson (D–Texas), agreed, and the incident was dropped.[23]

On the Senate side, Scripps-Howard reporter Seth Kantor was called to testify before the Senate Permanent Subcommittee on Investigations. Kantor had written an article which accurately predicted the winner of the TFX warplane contract a month before the award was made. Kantor would not name his sources for the story. He told the subcommittee that he would like to cooperate, but that he had pledged himself to confidentiality. The subcommittee did not pursue the matter, and the investigation ended.[24]

In 1971 the Special Subcommittee on Investigations of the House Committee on Interstate and Foreign Commerce conducted an investigation of the highly controversial CBS News television documentary "The Selling of the Pentagon." In the course of the investigation, the subcommittee subpoenaed CBS president Frank Stanton, asking him to bring all materials used in creating the program. Dr. Stanton agreed to provide tapes of the program as it was shown on the air. But he refused to give the subcommittee any of the "outtakes"—the unused material gathered in preparing the documentary. The subcommittee voted to cite CBS for contempt—and it brought the matter to the House floor. On July 13, 1971, the House voted 226–181 to recommit the motion to the committee, thus killing the move to find CBS in contempt.[25]

In 1972 the Tennessee State Senate tried to force a newsman to name his sources for a story in the Memphis (Tennessee) *Commercial Appeal*. Reporter Joseph Weiler was assigned to investigate reports that retarded children were being mistreated at Arlington Hospital, a state-operated hospital for the retarded. Weiler's investigation confirmed the reports.

"Once we thought we could prove it, we went to the hospital administration," said Weiler. "They confirmed it was true. There were numerous cases of child abuse. Eight persons already had been fired. None of this had been made public."[26] On July 20, 1972, the *Commercial Appeal* published Weiler's story on the hospital scandal. Another employee was fired, and more than a dozen others were reprimanded and suspended.

In September 1972 the Tennessee State Senate Committee on General Welfare and Environment began an investigation into the matter. However, as Representative Dan Kuykendall (R–Tenn.) observed, "curiously, the state senators zeroed in *not* on the child beaters, but on the reporter who had dared bring this condition to public light. They hauled Joe Weiler in front of them, and told him to bring all of his notes and correspondence with him."[27]

Weiler was called to testify on the second day of the hearings. He appeared without a lawyer. "I was scared," said the twenty-five-year old journalist. "The committee members had stated publicly their main purpose was getting the sources and the newsmen so they could stop the publicity. They said we were creating a disturbance at the hospital, and we were responsible for the continued uproar out there by publishing these stories. We felt the problem wasn't the uproar being created but child abuse."[28]

Later on the second day of the hearings, Weiler returned with a lawyer, who offered a compromise: Weiler would agree to turn over information to the committee as long as he could withhold information that might reveal his sources. The committee wanted the sources, however, and voted unanimously to give Weiler thirty days to show why he should not be held in contempt. If found in contempt, his sentence could have ranged from ten days to six months in jail.

Meanwhile, the state senate committee subpoenaed a local radio newsman, Joe Pennington of WREC, who had broadcast a similar story about the hospital. Behind the committee's closed doors Pennington revealed his source to the committee: a secretary at Arlington Hospital. The secretary was suspended immediately from her job, even though she denied her role in the matter.

Weiler, however, continued to maintain the confidentiality of his source. A confrontation and court battle was avoided when the Tennessee attorney general was asked to rule whether the senate committee was legally constituted after the November 7 election. The attorney general ruled that the committee was not so constituted. The threat of a jail term for Joe Weiler had ended.

"I have maintained throughout," said Weiler, "that the free press in the United States has the right to perform its duties without fear or intimidation, and I hope that right at last will be enacted into law when the state legislature convenes next month."[29]

In addition to being subpoenaed by Congress and state legislatures, reporters also have been subpoenaed by departments and agencies of the federal government. However, the agencies and departments have been more reluctant to battle with journalists.

In 1966, for example, newspaper reports indicated several weeks before the official announcement was made that the government was going to expand the U.S. soybean crop. Some speculators apparently made money as a result of their early knowledge. Reporters covering the Agriculture Department were asked by a department investigator to tell "how they handled the story, where and when they received the information," and other details.[30] The reporters told the investigator that the information requested was confidential, and that they would not cooperate. The Inspector General of the Agriculture Department, Lester Condon, said the agency respected the decision of the journalists to maintain their confidential sources, and the issue was dropped.

In 1971 syndicated columnist Arthur Rowse praised Representative Fred Rooney (D–Pa.) for conducting a "lonely crusade" that eventually spurred the Federal Trade Commission to take action against allegedly misleading sales tactics by magazine publishers. In the course of adjudicating charges against the Hearst Corporation, FTC examiner John Poindexter was asked by Hearst's lawyers to subpoena documents, notes and other materials used by Rowse in preparing his article. Hearst's defense was based partly on the contention that the commission acted only at the behest of Representative Rooney.

The subpoena was served on Rowse, who immediately moved to have it quashed on the grounds that it violated his constitutional rights. The reporter said that divulging his unpublished notes and information "would severely handicap my continued ability to gather news and keep the public informed on issues in this vital area."[31] Rowse's motion was granted by Poindexter on the grounds that the material sought from Rowse was not necessary for Hearst's defense, because it was not improper for a Congressman to urge that FTC proceedings be undertaken.[32]

Clearly, the confrontations the press has had with the Congress, state legislatures and administrative agencies have varied in many respects. Nevertheless, there are some striking similarities, which point toward four general observations.

First, articles that have provoked subpoenas have contained allegations of official corruption or misconduct, or have been stories officials did not want the public to read, for one reason or another.

Second, legislative bodies and administrative agencies have not been concerned so much with the substance of journalistic exposés as with "who spilled the beans." The rationale for subpoenaing reporters has been motivated by vindictiveness against a reporter or his sources rather than by a sincere legislative interest in a substantive problem.

Third, in almost every instance journalists have refused to reveal their sources.

Fourth, in many cases, the legislative branch and administrative agencies have been reluctant to follow through with sanctions against reporters who refuse to divulge information. This probably is due largely to legislators' sensitivity to public opinion. It is significant, however, that a reporter's right to withhold information has not been recognized officially. His position has been, and remains, a precarious one, balanced between the whims of often hostile legislators and an outraged public.

3

Journalists
Do Not Always Lose
But Sometimes They Talk

MOST OF THE BATTLES between the government and the press have occurred in courtrooms rather than in Congressional or legislative chambers. Unlike Congress, state legislatures and administrative agencies, the courts have not been reluctant to use their power of punishment for contempt for refusals to reveal subpoenaed information.

When a reporter is summoned to testify before a court or grand jury about confidential information, there are three possible results: (1) the reporter is able to maintain the confidentiality of his information without being charged with contempt; (2) the reporter divulges his source of information; and (3) the reporter maintains his confidences and is sentenced for contempt.

In this chapter, cases involving the first two results will be examined: those where the reporter successfully shields his sources, and those where the reporter talks.

REPORTER MAINTAINS CONFIDENCE
WITHOUT PENALTY

In the absence of a state statute establishing a testimonial privilege for reporters, cases where journalists have
been able to maintain the confidentiality of their sources
or information and yet not be punished for contempt have
been infrequent—but they have occurred. In virtually every
instance, however, the reporter's success has *not* been based
on a First Amendment legal privilege for journalists.

On New Year's Eve, 1913, a front-page story in the
New York Tribune reported that Lucius Littauer, a
wealthy former Congressman, and Mrs. W. Ellis Corey,
wife of a former president of the U.S. Steel Corporation,
were being investigated on charges of smuggling jewelry
into the country.

George Burdick, the city editor of the *Tribune*, and a
ship-news reporter, William Curtin, were called before a
grand jury investigating customs fraud. The grand jury demanded the source of the information in the article. Both
Burdick and Curtin refused to comply—but not on the
ground of journalists' privilege. Instead, they pleaded the
Fifth Amendment, arguing that answering the question
might tend to incriminate them. In response, President Wil-
son offered them pardons for any offense they might have
committed in connection with the fraud.

But both Burdick and Curtin continued to refuse to
name their source, which makes it seem probable that they
chose the "Fifth" as a surer means of protection than the
assertion of a reporter's "privilege," since it was a certainty
that the latter would not have been recognized judicially.

The Federal District Court held the reporters in contempt, fining them $500 each. The Supreme Court, how-
ever, heard the case on appeal and reversed the decision.[1]
The point of law the decision turned on was not a reporter's
privilege, but whether or not a pardon could be refused.

The Court ruled that since a pardon carried an imputation of guilt it was not valid unless accepted. The reporters were thus off the hook. (Meanwhile, Littauer and Mrs. Corey were successfully prosecuted.)

In 1933 a newsman declined to testify in civil court on the ground that he might lose his job if he divulged the requested information. Frank Toughill, a *Philadelphia Record* reporter, had written a story indicating that a secret hearing of the State Alcohol Permit Board had resulted in approval of a permit for a particular distilling company. The permit was rescinded after the article was published.

In a suit brought by the distilling company to force the board to reissue the permit, Toughill was called as a witness. He was asked where he received his information. He refused to cooperate, claiming that if he did so his employment would be jeopardized. The court did not compel him to answer.

In that same year, *San Diego Union* newsman William Cayce left unanswered a grand-jury attempt to learn the source of his information regarding a murder case. The grand jury recommended that the Superior Court hold the journalist in contempt. But the Superior Court dismissed the order against Cayce. The ruling was based on the ground that the questions were irrelevant, since the grand jury had already completed its work and secured an indictment.

In 1934 a famous case was heard in Chicago after *Chicago American* reporter A.L. Sloan wrote a series of pieces exposing wrongdoing in the Illinois Emergency Relief Commission.

While Sloan refused to identify his informants for the series before a grand jury, he did agree to give the jury the names of fifteen people who *could* provide additional information about the graft charges. The grand jury nonetheless recommended that he be cited for contempt.

A ten-day contempt hearing was conducted. As the *Chicago American* editorialized:

> The proposition being decided was the case of the *Chicago American*, representing the public, against grafters and thieves in the operations of the Illinois Emergency Relief Commission with $170,000,000 of public funds, but what developed seemed to be the case of Judge Finnegan, the state's attorney's office, and the grand jury against the *Chicago American* for exposing all the graft.[2]

Chief Justice Philip Finnegan of the Criminal Court finally dropped the charges. He concluded that the information sought from the reporter was not particularly relevant, and that Sloan would never reveal the information anyway:

> If the court were satisfied that Sloan had facts which might lead to the proof of graft, fraud, payroll padding, and other criminal acts, the ends of justice could possibly be served by a commitment order, the effect of which might tend to bring those facts to light, either from Sloan or from others with whom he may have had contact. The record indicates, however, that the state's attorney, the grand jury, and the court can be more profitably employed than living in the hope or expectation of substantial proofs from Sloan in his present state of declamatory but uninformed zeal.[3]

One year after the Sloan case, a writer for the *Brooklyn Eagle* was summoned in a trial of four members of a New York gang. The reporter, T. Norman Palmer, had covered the police investigations of the hoodlums for the *Eagle*. Judge Charles S. Colden, in the Queens County Court, Long Island City, New York, excused Palmer on the basis of the right to keep confidential the names of informants:

. . . this court recognizes the right of a newspaperman to refrain from divulging sources of his information. If you feel that in doing this (taking the stand), it may interfere with this right, you are at liberty not to take the stand at this time.[4]

A similar ruling was made in a lower court in Tennessee in 1948. The *Nashville Tennesseean* had printed a series of articles claiming that policemen were involved in a local liquor racket. Nat Caldwell, the reporter who wrote the stories, was called before the Anderson County (Tennessee) grand jury, where he refused to state his sources of information. According to the grand jury, Caldwell should have been cited for contempt.

But the County Circuit Court ruled that Caldwell was not in contempt for maintaining the confidentiality of his informants:

> The press must get its information through others, of necessity much is given in confidence, and I am unable to hold the witness in contempt in this matter. It's true it's hard to have charges made against a public official on hearsay evidence, but at times much good has been done in that way.[5]

In 1951 a federal court held that a journalist did not have to reveal information—but only because it was not considered relevant to the matter at hand. After Ethel Rosenberg was convicted of treason, reporter Leonard Lyons wrote a series about death row in the *New York Post*. Lyons included in his syndicated material indications that Mrs. Rosenberg's death sentence could be altered if she decided to talk, and Mrs. Rosenberg tried to force Lyons to reveal his sources for that contention. The court ruled that Lyons did not have to answer the questions because they were not relevant to the proceedings. But the court also noted that "a newspaper correspondent must answer pertinent questions and disclose the sources of his information that he has published or caused to be published if the questions be relevant to the proceeding in which the questions are asked."[6]

In 1969 *St. Paul Dispatch* reporter Donald Giese was asked by the defendant's lawyer in a murder trial to reveal where he got the information for the articles he had written about the killing. Giese steadfastly resisted. He said:

> I think that this deprives me of my right to confidential news sources and my right to keep those confidential news sources; and, two, it tends to violate the basic ethics of my profession; and, three, it tends to deprive me of property without due process of law in violation of the Fourteenth Amendment to the United States Constitution.[7]

The trial court found Giese in contempt of court and sentenced him to ninety days in the county jail. The Minnesota Supreme Court overturned the conviction, because it considered the question asked of Giese irrelevant to the defendant's case. "In post-conviction proceedings," said the court, "there must be a real basis for the examination of witnesses, and the examination must focus upon a concrete claim of prejudice or denial of a constitutional right."[8]

In 1970 a Circuit Court judge in Chicago and a U.S. District Court judge in New York refused to compel journalists to testify about their confidential sources.

In Chicago the defense counsel for nineteen Weathermen asked that reporters be required to testify and produce transcripts of all their reports of activities concerning the SDS (Students for a Democratic Society) group. The SDS members had been charged with a variety of offenses. Circuit Court Judge Saul Epton ruled that the reporters did not have to comply with the defense attorney's request:

It is true the defendants have a clear right to subpoena individuals who have knowledge of relevant facts. However, the First Amendment is as sacred as the Sixth Amendment, and if the press is to be free, they cannot be disturbed unnecessarily in reporting or gathering materials to report.[9]

In New York two journalists were subpoenaed to testify at a hearing on a suit filed by the federal government and the Air Transport Association of America against the Professional Air Traffic Control Organization. The government and the ATA were seeking to have PATCO cited for contempt for failing to comply with a restraining order. The ATA attorney asked Robert Lindsey, a *New York Times* reporter, if he kept notes of conversations with PATCO officials. Lindsey's attorney objected to the question on the ground that releasing the notes would be an invasion of privacy and a violation of the First Amendment. U.S. District Judge Orrin Judd sustained the *Times'* objection, ruling:

I have taken lots of statements, even in criminal cases, where notes have been destroyed. You're dealing with the news media, and I'm not going to require the production of notes. You have had ample cross-examination.[10]

On August 13, 1972, the *Columbia* (South Carolina) *State* published a story by reporter Hugh Munn documenting irregularities at the county jail. Munn had interviewed four prisoners in the county jail, pledging that he would not reveal their names so that they would not face reprisals from prison authorities, and took sworn affidavits from them. The prisoners talked about guards propositioning the inmates' wives, with the implication that if the women did not accept the propositions, their husbands would receive tougher treatment. The prisoners also told of beatings and other infractions by prison authorities.

Fifth Circuit Solicitor John Foard was angered by the revelations and warned members of the news media that the Supreme Court had ruled that reporters do not have a constitutional right to withhold their sources. "We are not here today to deal with students writing for a university newspaper," Foard said. "We are dealing with one large corporation—the *State* newspaper—and with adults over 21 . . . If those names are not furnished to me promptly, this time we are going to the Grand Jury, and we really mean business."[11]

The *State* agreed to provide the affidavits in their entirety with one exception: the names would be deleted. Nevertheless, managing editor Robert Pierce and city editor Thomas McLean were subpoenaed, along with Munn, by the Richland County grand jury.

Managing editor Pierce commented that it was "curious that the solicitor would concentrate on the incidental matter of how the newspaper came about its information rather than on the prime issues raised."[12] The *State* editorialized that, "Surely, Richland authorities are competent to investigate a little matter at their own jail. Is further involvement by our newsmen 'a legitimate need of law enforcement'?"

The *State* editors and Munn gave the grand jury the affidavits without the names on them. The grand jury decided not to pursue the matter. (Incidentally, the investigation into the prison irregularities produced no indictments.)

It was the second time that the *State* had faced a subpoena for confidential sources. An earlier case involved reporter Luke West, who did a story on corruption in a county government in conjunction with the *Florence Morning News*. The grand jury subpoenaed West, but he refused to reveal his information, telling the jurors to read the articles instead. The grand jury did not pursue the matter.

In December 1972 two *Los Angeles Times* reporters and the *Times'* Washington Bureau chief were subpoenaed and asked to turn over tapes of conversations with a witness in the Watergate case, the break-in and bugging of the Democratic National Committee office in Washington, D. C. The reporters—Jack Nelson and Ronald Ostrow—indicated that they would "never" turn over records of an interview with witness Alfred C. Baldwin III unless Baldwin authorized it. "It goes to the point of nobody's ever going to believe us again, nobody's ever going to talk to us again. I might as well go into a different line of work," said Ostrow, indicating the effects of revealing the information.[13] Bureau chief John Lawrence likewise refused to turn over the tapes. Since Nelson and Ostrow had given the tapes of the five-hour interview with Baldwin to the *Times*, Lawrence was jailed for contempt of court on December 19 as a representative of the *Times*. U. S. District Court Chief Judge John J. Sirica's ruling was stayed by the U. S. Court of Appeals and Lawrence was freed two hours after he was jailed, pending an appeal of Sirica's ruling.

The case ended abruptly two days later when Baldwin came to the reporters' rescue and released the *Times* from its pledge of confidentiality. The tapes were turned over to the court and the reporters were released from contempt charges.

Also in December 1972 another Los Angeles newsman became embroiled in a subpoena controversy. Reporter Jim Mitchell of KFWB radio conducted a series of interviews concerning a bail-bond scandal in Los Angeles. One of the interviews was with Superior Court Judge Leopoldo Sanchez, one of three judges accused of signing blank prisoner-release forms and furnishing them to bail bondsmen.

A Los Angeles County grand jury ordered Mitchell to produce notes and tapes of his interviews, regardless of whether the material had been broadcast. Art Schreiber, general manager of the station, said that the station would provide material which had been broadcast, but that unused material "raised serious First Amendment questions."[14]

Schreiber attempted to quash the subpoena, but he was unsuccessful. However, the grand jury did not charge Schreiber or Mitchell with contempt. The grand jury's term expired on December 31, 1972, and it therefore no longer had the power to sanction the reporters or the station. There is a possibility, however, that a new grand jury will be formed. Schreiber has declared that he will continue to refuse to turn over unused tape if called again. "I just can't do that," he said. "I think we destroy freedom of the press in the United States by serving as an arm of the government."[15]

Three cases decided in late 1972 indicated that reporters may not have to talk if the requested information is not relevant or necessary to a criminal investigation or case. The courts ruled that some "fishing expeditions" would not be sanctioned.

In 1970 two journalists for the Black Panther newspaper had refused to answer questions propounded by a federal grand jury investigating the Black Panthers. The questions posed to Sherrie Bursey and Brenda Presley concerned the operations of the newspaper, such as who made the assignments, who took photographs, and who did the layout. On June 30, 1972, the Ninth Circuit Court of Appeals reversed the contempt citations for the two newswomen, ruling that questions about the internal management of the newspaper raised First Amendment concerns and were not relevant or necessary for the investigation. A government request for a rehearing was denied on October 5, 1972.

Three *Milwaukee Sentinel* reporters were subpoenaed in October 1972. Gene Cunningham, Dean Jensen and Stuart Wilk had investigated Richard Nowakowski, the chairman of the county board of supervisors, and the allegations that he had obtained improper favors from contractors who did business for the county.

After a grand jury began to investigate Nowakowski, he himself filed a suit in federal District Court seeking an injunction against the grand jury. During the pretrial proceedings, the three reporters were ordered to disclose their information. The reporters refused and appealed to the Court of Appeals for a stay. The stay was granted, with the court pointing out that Nowakowski had to demonstrate some substance to his claim before the reporters would be compelled to testify.

And in December 1972 the Second Circuit Court of Appeals ruled that Alfred Balk, editor of the *Columbia Journalism Review*, did not have to identify a source he used in a 1962 article for the *Saturday Evening Post*.

Plaintiffs in a civil-rights class action (that is, a case in which one plaintiff represents a whole group or class that is similarly aggrieved) in behalf of Chicago blacks had sought an order to compel Balk to name his source for the article, which concerned racial discrimination in real estate. The source, fictitiously called "Norris Vitchek" in the article, presumably would have been used as evidence in a case against Chicago real estate operators. However, the information was requested from Balk in pretrial proceedings, and the plaintiffs had not sought to learn the true identity of "Vitchek" except by questioning Balk. The court said that the Supreme Court's ruling in *Branzburg v. Hayes* (that reporters did *not* have a First Amendment right to withhold information from grand juries) was based on subpoenaed information in criminal proceedings, and that "there are circumstances, at the very least in civil cases," in which reporters would not be forced to reveal information.

Thus, there have been instances where reporters have

refused to reveal information and escaped punishment. But only a few of these have been based on a First Amendment privilege for journalists—and those were overruled in *Branzburg v. Hayes* (discussed in Chapter 5). Although some courts have recently held that reporters are not required to reveal information if there is no apparent need for it, the Supreme Court's ruling that there is no First Amendment right for journalists to refuse to comply with a subpoena is the law today. In short, the "victories" cited here have been individual successes. They have not strengthened the position of other journalists or freedom of the press in general.

THE REPORTER TALKS

In rare instances, members of the press have submitted to the court rather than accept punishment for contempt.

In 1914 a city editor in Hawaii printed a story about local government corruption prior to the official release of the information by a grand jury. The editor refused to name his informant in court, claiming privilege as a journalist. The District Court denied the claim:

> The position of the witness is untenable. Though there is a canon of journalistic ethics forbidding the disclosure of a newspaper's source of information—a canon worthy of respect and undoubtedly well-founded, it is subject to qualification—it must yield when in conflict with the interests involved of justice—the private interests involved must yield to the interests of the public.[16]

The court viewed legal privilege as a personal one for the reporter rather than as one for providing the public with a wider range of information. After the court ruled against the reporter, he revealed his source.

In 1931 two organizers in Dallas, Texas, began making speeches in favor of racial equality. C.J. Coder and Leads Hurst were later incarcerated on a charge of vagrancy and allegedly beaten by policemen in the jail.

Dallas Dispatch writer Eddie Barr wrote that Coder and Hurst had been kidnaped and flogged and that their lawyer had also been kidnaped. According to Barr's account, attorney George Edwards was warned not to represent Coder and Hurst. Barr was summoned before a grand jury but would not disclose his sources. He was fined a hundred dollars and was sent to jail for contempt of court.

Barr's attorney advised him that he could gain his freedom only if he purged himself of contempt by supplying the identification. Barr agreed to name his source in open court. He said it was the chief clerk in the office of the district attorney who put Barr in jail!

In 1961 *Duluth Labor World* reporter Curt Miller wrote that the *Northern Venture*, a Canadian cargo ship, would be picketed by the Seafarers International Union. The Seafarers claimed that a Candian union—the Canadian Brotherhood of Railway, Transportation and General Workers—was taking away jobs and forcing men to work under unfavorable conditions.

The attorney for the Canadian union filed a motion for an injunction to end the picketing, and in a hearing on the injunction request the lawyer asked Federal District Court Judge Sidney Kaner to compel Miller to reveal the name of his source. Judge Kaner ordered Miller to testify, observing that if reporters were to have the privilege of withholding sources, "the legislature would have passed a law similar to those for doctors, lawyers, and clergymen."[17] Miller told the court the name of the man whose information was used in the article.

In 1967 two Arkansas reporters discovered that legislators had been offered a thousand dollars each to vote for a bill to legalize casino gambling at private clubs in Hot Springs. Jack Baker of the *Arkansas Gazette* and Michael Smith of the *Pine Bluff Commercial* initially would not divulge the identities of their informants. However, to avoid a jail sentence for contempt, Smith changed his stance: "Since our informants had agreed to let us testify, I told the judge their names," he said.[18]

4

The Invariable
Courtroom Result:
The Reporter Loses

OCCASIONALLY REPORTERS have successfully shielded
their sources without being charged with contempt, and
several times journalists have agreed to disclose confidential
information. Most often, however, reporters have fought for
the right to keep secret the identities of their informants,
lost, and suffered the penalty for contempt of court.

The cases reporters have lost can be categorized on the
basis of the type of information involved: (1) libel cases,
in which a reporter has allegedly libeled someone; (2)
secret-information cases, in which a reporter has printed a
story containing official secrets; (3) crime and corruption
cases, in which a reporter has reported and revealed wrongdoing; and (4) sociological cases, in which a reporter has
printed information about groups or cultures little known
to the larger society.

LIBEL CASES

In 1886 a reporter for *The Defiance* in Atlanta, Georgia, wrote a story indicating that a real estate agent had forced a black man to move and sell at a loss. The article recommended that blacks rent houses from other agents and leave "this old skunk to himself to stink himself to death."[1] The publisher of *The Defiance* refused to testify in the libel case brought by the real estate agent named in the article, or to reveal the name of the writer of the story.

The Georgia Supreme Court sustained the trial court's contempt conviction against the publisher, observing that he knew "in advance that he might be placed in a perilous position, so he refused stubbornly . . . to testify at all. He surely merited the punishment he received." (The publisher's "merited punishment" was a $50 fine and ten days in jail.)[2]

Only recently, however, have libel cases involving the assertion of a privilege occurred with any frequency, and the privilege has been denied even in states with statutory privileges for reporters. Two instances in New Jersey indicate the courts' reluctance to allow a privilege in libel cases even if it is normally permitted. (New Jersey enacted a privilege statute in 1933.)

In April 1954 managing editor Allen Smith wrote an article for the *Passaic Herald-News* which stated that Clifton City Council candidate William Brogan was involved in a fistfight with another man the day before. Brogan took the newspaper to court, and it was determined at the trial that the story was not factual. Nevertheless, the newspaper's defense was based on the "reliability of the confidential informant." The New Jersey Supreme Court ruled that if the defense was based on "reliability of the source, the newspaper could not refuse to identify the source despite the existence of a state privilege law":

> The position of the respondents in this case is that they insist on asserting these defenses based upon the reliability of the source of information upon which they relied, yet refuse to disclose what those sources were, so that the jury could ascertain whether they were in fact reliable.
>
> A newspaper ought not to be able to give and take what it chooses when its own acts bring into question a liability on its part to others. If permitted to do as the defendant has here, the newspaper could give whatever information was favorable to its position and then plead the privilege to prevent any disclosure of the detrimental facts.[3]

The court pointed out that recovery for damages would be impossible if a newspaper could libel and then defend on the basis that the information came from a "reliable source" but refuse to disclose the identity of the source.

A similar case was heard by the Superior Court of New Jersey eight years later. The *Point Pleasant Leader* published an editorial in July 1963 which was critical of the police chief of Point Pleasant. The chief brought a libel action against the newspaper. The court relied on the Brogan case to rule that the privilege could not be invoked if the defendants simultaneously argued that the source was "reliable."[4]

The most famous libel case involving privilege occurred in 1959, when actress Judy Garland brought CBS to District Court for breach of contract and for defamatory statements. The statements, attributed to a CBS executive, were published in Marie Torre's column, "TV-Radio Today," in the January 10, 1957, issue of the *New York Herald Tribune*. Miss Torre quoted a CBS spokesman as saying that Miss Garland did not wish to work on a program she had agreed to do. The column concluded with the spokesman's alleged statement: "I don't know, but I wouldn't be surprised if it's because she thinks she's terribly fat." Miss

Garland claimed that the statements were false and damaging to her reputation; CBS claimed that it had never made the statements or caused them to be published.

In pretrial discovery proceedings, Marie Torre testified that the statements were the "exact words" of a CBS informant. She refused, however, to disclose the name of the source, asserting that she would violate a confidence if she did so. Proceedings were therefore initiated to compel her to reveal her source. She was held in contempt and appealed.

In her appeal she argued that forcing her to disclose the name of her source would inhibit the free flow of news and thereby restrict freedom of the press. In claiming explicit protection under the First Amendment, Miss Torre became the first reporter to rely specifically on the First Amendment as a rationale for a testimonial privilege.

Neither the time nor the type of case was right for such an argument, however. The Second Circuit Court of Appeals upheld the contempt charges. The court agreed that some restraint on the press would result from forced disclosure of sources, but it contended that no liberties were absolute. Miss Torre tried to appeal to the U.S. Supreme Court, but the Court refused to hear the case.[5]

Five years after the Garland–Torre case, San Francisco Giant baseball star Orlando Cepeda brought a libel suit against Cowles Magazine and Broadcasting, Inc. The article in question, written by Timothy Cohane, appeared in the May 21, 1963, edition of *Look* magazine.

Although the trial was held in California, Cohane was ordered to make a deposition in New York City. He did so but refused, on the grounds that the information was given to him in confidence, to answer questions concerning the identity of Giant officials who allegedly made derogatory comments about Cepeda.

The Cepeda case presented two particularly difficult issues of legal interpretation.

First, the trial took place in a jurisdiction (California) that had a privilege law, whereas Cohane's statement was taken in a state (New York) which did *not* then recognize a privilege. In resolving the conflict, the federal District Court ruled that the California law would apply, in part because that state "had the strongest interest in, and the most contacts with, the pending cause of action."[6]

Second, California's privilege was extended specifically to persons employed or connected with a newspaper, wire service, radio station or television station. Neither the word "magazine" nor the word "periodical" was included in the California statute. Thus the court had to determine whether or not magazine writers fell within the parameters of the statute's coverage. The court ruled that Cohane was required to answer the questions posed to him because magazine reporters did *not* possess a privilege under the California law:

> Bearing in mind that a privilege recognized by law constitutes an exception to the general liability of all persons to testify to all matters, in analyzing the aforementioned statute the Court must be guided by the rule of strict statutory construction.[7]

In 1964 the U.S. Supreme Court rendered a landmark decision in the area of libel law in the case of *New York Times v. Sullivan*. The court ruled that a public official may recover damages "for a defamatory falsehood relating to his official conduct" only if he proves that "the statement was made with 'actual malice'—that is, with knowledge that it was false or with reckless disregard of whether it was false or not."[8]

The 1964 ruling has made it more difficult to maintain libel actions against reporters who have written critical stories about public officials. As a consequence, reporters may be more successful in future attempts to maintain the confidentiality of their sources in libel cases. (There were two cases pending in early 1973 on this issue.)

One court ruled that public officials may not use a libel suit as a simple means of discovering a reporter's confidential sources—malice must be proved before the disclosure of sources can be compelled.

For example, in May 1970 *Life* magazine published an article indicating that St. Louis Mayor Alfonso J. Cervantes maintained "business and personal ties with the gangsters that operate in his city." The article, titled "The Mayor, the Mob, and the Lawyer," described the relationship between Cervantes and underworld figures, which *Life* attempted to document.

Mayor Cervantes instituted a libel action for twelve million dollars against the publisher of *Life* and the reporter who wrote the article. The reporter testified during pretrial discovery proceedings that the basis of the article was derived from confidential information received from informants within the Federal Bureau of Investigation and the United States Department of Justice. But he refused, under repeated questioning, to reveal the names of the persons from whom he received the information.

The mayor moved for an order to compel the identity of the informants, but the District Court did not reach the motion to compel. Instead, it entered summary judgment for the defendants on the ground that "neither defendant had knowledge of falsity, that neither entertained serious doubts as to the truth of any statement in the article, and that neither acted with reckless disregard for truth or falsity."[9]

That decision was affirmed by the Eighth Circuit Court of Appeals, whose ruling stated that courts could not "routinely grant motions seeking compulsory disclosure of anonymous news sources without first inquiring into the substance of a libel allegation . . ."[10] The case was still pending appeal to the Supreme Court in early 1973.

A conflicting decision was rendered by federal District Court Judge Howard Corcoran, however, in a more recent libel case. A one-paragraph story appeared in Jack Anderson's syndicated column, which raised questions about a reported burglary at the headquarters of the United Mine Workers. U.M.W. lawyer Edward Carey filed a nine-million-dollar libel suit against Anderson, his associate Brit Hume and the *Washington Post*, which carried the column.

Judge Corcoran ordered Hume to name his confidential sources for the story, but Hume refused. The case was appealed to the U.S. Circuit Court of Appeals for Washington, D.C., and was still pending in January 1973.[11]

The legal concepts in the area of libel are still developing. It is clear that if malice is established, a reporter can be forced to reveal his confidential sources. However, the Eighth Circuit Court of Appeals ruling that a reporter cannot be forced to talk unless such a showing is made cannot yet be considered "good" law. The final resolution awaits the action of the courts.

SECRET-INFORMATION CASES

The law has not looked with tolerance on journalists who have published legal secrets obtained through confidential sources.

In 1896 the *Baltimore Sun* published information about particular actions the city grand jury was going to take. John Morris, the reporter, was immediately called before the grand jury. Asked to name the source of his information, he refused, despite warnings that he would be held in contempt. The grand jury recommended to the presiding judge that Morris be jailed. The judge, however, decided not to accept the recommendation because the contempt, if it had occurred, had not occurred in his court. The grand jury then acted on its own, and in an unprecedented step, assumed the power to send Morris to jail for five days. The grand jury's term ended after five days, and Morris was released.

The *Sun* did not end its campaign for legal protection for reporters, and the campaign proved to be effective. Two months after the Morris case, Maryland enacted the first reporters' privilege statute in the United States. The statute, still in force today, provides that a person "engaged in, connected with or employed by" a newspaper cannot be "compelled to disclose" in any legal proceeding "the source of news or information."

An article similar to Morris', revealing information about the secret grand-jury proceedings, was written by *Seattle Star* reporter Lester Hunt in 1939. The grand jury demanded that Hunt disclose his sources. He not only refused but continued to write articles about the grand-jury deliberations.

Hunt was held in contempt for "refusing to answer certain questions propounded to him by the grand jury on May 18" and for writing an article the day after he refused to reveal his sources. Superior Judge D. F. Wright declared:

> An article flaunting the court and grand jury appeared in the Seattle paper today, under authorship of Hunt, which in itself is a revelation of certain matters and things that occurred before the grand jury, which are secret and privileged and contrary to the oath of the witness.[12]

Hunt was sentenced to ten days in jail.

In 1950 Reuben Clein published articles in *Miami Life* concerning activities that took place in the grand-jury room. Called before the grand jury, he refused to answer questions that would reveal his source, citing the journalists' code of ethics as his reason. The grand jury recommended prosecution for contempt, and the Florida Supreme Court upheld the recommendation in a contempt proceeding.

A complex case involving the release of "secret" information arose out of the sensational Charles Manson murder trial in 1970. Prior to the trial, Los Angeles Superior Court Judge William Keene signed an "Order re Publicity" prohibiting any attorney, court employee or witness from publicly releasing the contents of any testimony that might be given in order, according to Judge Older, who was hearing the case, to prevent prejudicial publicity that might keep the defendants from receiving a fair trial. (This kind of order was authorized by American Bar Association ethical rules adopted in 1969. At that time it was emphasized that the rules "would give judges new powers only over lawyers, not newsmen."[13])

Reporter William Farr covered the trial for the *Los Angeles Herald-Examiner* and spent several months attempting to get information in the possession of Virginia Graham, a potential witness in the case. On October 7, 1970, Farr received two copies of a written statement by Miss Graham, one each from two of the six attorneys in the case. The next day he obtained a third copy from another person subject to the Order re Publicity but not an attorney of record.

The trial judge, Superior Court Judge Charles Older, was informed by Miss Graham's lawyer that Farr had a copy of her statement. On October 8, 1970, Judge Older conducted a hearing in his chambers to ascertain if Farr had the statement and, if he did, the identity of the persons who gave it to him. Farr voluntarily attended the hearing and told the judge that he had obtained the statement from two of the attorneys. He added that he did not have control over what happened to the story about the statement because the city editor made publication decisions. And relying on the California shield statute, he refused to identify his sources by name. The judge dropped the matter.

The *Herald-Examiner* decided to publish Farr's article on October 9, 1970. On the night of October 8, after publication was set, Farr called Judge Older to warn him so that the judge could take measures to prevent the jury from seeing the headlines while riding the bus from their sequestered hotel to the courtroom.

The October 9 story was headlined, "Liz, Sinatra on Slay List—Tate Witness." The account related the gory details of the murders planned by the Manson family. In Miss Graham's statement she indicated that defendant Susan Atkins had told her how Manson had planned to murder a series of show-business personalities.

The jury did not see the article.

When the trial finally ended, Manson and three women co-defendants were convicted of murdering Sharon Tate and six other persons. The issue seemed closed.

In May 1971 the matter of Farr refusing to reveal his sources was reopened. Judge Older learned that Farr was no longer a working journalist, having taken a job as press secretary for the district attorney of Los Angeles County, and issued an order requiring Farr to show cause why he should not be required to reveal his sources.

At the "show cause" hearing, Farr declared that "within hours after the discovery of the bodies of the deceased persons . . . I was assigned . . . to cover this case, and from that time until my resignation from the *Herald-Examiner* to on or about February 26, 1971, I covered [the Manson trial] on a full time basis . . ." Farr also said that he "obtained from confidential sources a transcript of one Virginia Graham," and that he gave his "explicit promise to said sources" that he "would never divulge the source."[14]

Farr was again asked by Judge Older at the hearing to name his sources. He continued to refuse:

> Notwithstanding my change of employment, I still feel
> bound in conscience to the ethics of my profession and
> my responsibility to my former employer to maintain the
> same position, to wit: To invoke the provisions of Sec-
> tion 1070 of the Evidence Code [California shield law].
> To do otherwise in my opinion would be to violate the
> ethics of my profession, the law of California and my
> own conscience. To violate my word and that of my
> former employer would destroy my relationships in my
> present position, would cause me irrevocable damage in
> the future and would prevent me from ever obtaining
> employment with another newspaper, news service or
> radio or TV station.[15]

Judge Older ruled that since Farr was no longer a reporter, the California shield law did not apply and found
him guilty of contempt. He suspended the sentence, however, pending appeal.

In December 1971 the California Court of Appeals affirmed the conviction. The court did not reach the issue of
whether or not the California statute still applied to Farr.
It held that regardless of the statute, granting immunity to
Farr "would be to countenance an unconstitutional interference by the legislative branch with an inherent and vital
power of the court to control its own proceedings and officers."[16]

The court observed that unless Farr was forced to name
the lawyers who violated the court publicity order, such
orders could never be enforced and would be meaningless:

> The trial court was enjoined by controlling precedent of
> the United States Supreme Court to take reasonable ac-

tion to protect the defendants in the Manson case from the effects of prejudicial publicity. It performed its duty by issuing the Order re Publicity. By petitioner's [Farr's] own statement that order was violated by two attorneys of record, of a list of six counsel in the case. Those attorneys were officers of respondent court. By petitioner's own statement the violations occurred because of his solicitation. Respondent court was both bound and empowered to explore the violations of its order by its own officers.[17]

The California Supreme Court denied Farr's appeal, and on November 13, 1972, the U.S. Supreme Court denied Farr's petition for certiorari, thus refusing to hear the case.

On November 16, 1972, Judge Older conducted another hearing and once more asked Farr to name his source. When he refused, the judge ordered him to jail "until such time as he will answer each and every question."[18] (The judge had asked thirteen specific questions, each naming a potential source and asking Farr for confirmation.)

Farr spent four hours in jail and was released on a writ of habeas corpus contending that Judge Older had lost jurisdiction in the case a year after the Manson trial ended. The appeal was rejected, and Farr was returned to jail on November 17, 1972, by Judge Older, who branded the reporter as a "martyr without a cause."[19]

This time Farr spent forty-eight days in jail before he was released by U.S. Supreme Court Justice William O. Douglas on January 11, 1973. Justice Douglas released Farr until a final ruling was made on another habeas corpus petition. But if the Ninth Circuit Court of Appeals finally rules against him on the petition, Farr will be sent to jail for an indefinite term.

The Farr case is unusual in a number of respects.

First, the contents of the article did not provide the public with vital information about government corruption or important societal issues. In fact, Farr and the *Herald-Examiner* were criticized by much of the journalistic community for their judgment. ("It seems to us," editorialized the *New Republic*, "that the newspaper erred by rushing into print with a seamy sensational account based on material obtained in contradiction to court order, and where the selling of more newspapers was the only public service rendered."[20] And the *New York Times* observed that "the sensationalized treatment given to the Manson trial by much of the press reflected little credit on journalism's own record of concern for assuring fair trial.")[21]

Second, the fact that Farr was no longer a reporter when he was subpoenaed provided a loophole whereby the courts, in effect, circumvented the California shield statute. (The statute was amended as a consequence of the Farr case to protect information received by journalists even after they retire or change jobs.)

Third, Farr obtained what was, in effect, a "secret" document. The "gag rule" imposed by the judge in the Manson case was designed to protect the defendants' constitutional rights to a fair trial, and the courts are justifiably concerned with protecting that right. Thus, in this case there was a countervailing interest that is not present in most cases.

Despite these unusual aspects, however, the *New York Times* astutely noted that "there is still great damage in the kind of remedy the courts are applying against Mr. Farr. The meanest cases often result in the most embracing and destructive trespasses on basic liberties."[22]

Although the courts are charged with, and must uphold, the responsibility to provide a fair trial for criminal defendants, they must not rely on reporters to enforce the rules they adopt. In the Farr case, the *Herald-Examiner* article was not seen by the jury and did not affect the trial. Two attorneys were apparently guilty of violating the Order re Publicity, and the court must attempt to bring those lawyers to justice. It cannot do so, however, by putting Farr behind bars.

The case embodies the entire free-press/fair-trial controversy that has raged for years and that cannot be adequately discussed within the confines of this book. Perhaps the best suggestion in resolving the Farr-case dilemma is for the court to place more emphasis on protecting defendants from publicity by ensuring that the jury is sequestered adequately instead of placing limitations—direct or indirect—on the press.

There are numerous debatable issues concerning the general problem of journalists' securing secret information, but one should be paramount: the press must not be coerced into abandoning its role as a check on government and government secrecy. Instead of discouraging reporters from ferreting out "secrets," the policy should be to encourage it. It is the responsibility of the federal and state governments to ensure that those few matters that require secrecy are kept secret. If a reporter manages to acquire such information, the government concerned should consider its security procedures a failure and attempt to strengthen them.

CRIME AND CORRUPTION CASES

Although confidential information has spawned an endless variety of articles in the press, it is most often used in stories exposing crime or corruption.

In 1897 defense attorneys for an individual accused of murder attempted to prohibit information from a conversation between the accused and a reporter from being introduced into evidence, invoking a reporter's privilege not to testify.

The prosecution asked the defendant if he had not told a

Miss Cunningham (the reporter) that he had seen the victim at the murder site and that the victim had been murdered there. At this point, the defendant's lawyers argued that communication between their client and Miss Cunningham was privileged because she was a journalist. This stretched the concept of reporters' privilege beyond recognition, however, and the argument was quickly dismissed; the court said the request "scarcely merits comment."[23]

In 1911 an *Augusta* (Georgia) *Herald* reporter was summoned to appear before a police board in the trial of a police officer. The reporter, Thomas Hamilton, had written a story about a murder on the basis of information received from a policeman. At the trial, Hamilton was asked to tell the board the name of the policeman. Hamilton refused, contending that he would lose his job if he disclosed his source. "It would ruin me in my business," he said, "it would cause me to lose my position as a newspaper reporter . . . and would prevent my ever engaging in the occupation of a newspaper reporter again."[24]

The police board fined Hamilton fifty dollars and sentenced him to prison until the fine was paid. Hamilton brought an action against the county jailer, and the case was heard by the Georgia Supreme Court. The court rejected Hamilton's arguments for a privilege.

> A promise not to testify when so required is substantially a promise not to obey the law. Such promises cannot be recognized, save in subordination to the requirements of the law. Neither can the wishes, or even the commands, of employers be allowed to outweigh the commands of the law . . . To sustain such a doctrine would render courts impotent and the effort to administer justice often times a mockery.[25]

In December 1911 a newspaperman for the *Jersey Journal* wrote an article which charged that a village trustee was corrupt. The newsman, Julius Grunow, did not deny that he had written the story, but he refused to disclose the name of his informant. "I was a newspaper reporter," he said later, "and therefore could not give up my sources of information."[26] The court, however, reasoned differently:

> In effect he pleaded a privilege which finds no countenance in the law. Such an immunity, as claimed by the defendant, would be far reaching in its effect and detrimental to the due administration of justice. To admit of any such privilege would be to shield the real transgressor and permit him to go unwhipped of justice.[27]

In 1929 three reporters for the *Washington Times*, Linton Burkett, Gorman Hendricks and John Nevin, published the results of their investigation of speakeasies operating in Washington, D.C., which indicated widespread violations of the prohibition law. Shortly thereafter, they were called by a grand jury seeking the names of the people who had sold them liquor. When they refused to give the information, they were sentenced to forty-five days in the District of Columbia jail.

"All of our information was gained in confidence insofar as the government was concerned," Burkett stated, "and we feel that to violate this confidence would be to violate professional ethics. If we gave the names and addresses of the men who sold us the liquor we would be placed in the position of prohibition agents, stool pigeons and snoopers."[28]

The three jailed reporters in the nation's capital spurred the first legislation introduced in Congress to protect reporters from forced disclosure of their sources.

Three years later, an intense confrontation between the press and the court flared up in the small town of Hopewell, Virginia. The trouble began in November 1931, when the editor of the *Hopewell News*, J. W. Mapoles, was fined ten dollars for contempt of court. Mapoles had printed an article about a liquor charge being dismissed in Judge Thomas Robinson's Hopewell corporation court. Judge Robinson also levied a ten-dollar fine on Hopewell police chief C.H. Shepherd because, according to the judge, the chief had led people to believe that the court had dismissed a "big bootlegger."

In December, seventeen of the town's twenty-four practicing attorneys signed a demurrer to the Shepherd order, protesting the judge's action. Judge Robinson was angered. "I am not going to sit here and submit to any such oppression as that of fifteen or twenty lawyers coming in here about nothing, making a fool of the court," he said.[29]

The next day, in addition to reports about the protest of the lawyers, the following letter appeared in the *Hopewell News*:

> Editor, *Hopewell News*:
> Dear Sir: What a ludicrous incident that was Friday. Sixteen lawyers all good and true, facing an irate court official (if facts were as reported in the *Daily Express*)!
>
> If sixteen efficient men of the Virginia bar, able and fluent, have no success in pleading a case, it looks like that many men might be "hefty" enough to remove the court bodily.
>
> —Jokester[30]

The letter was published with twelve others commenting on the case.

After appearing at several sessions of the grand jury, Mapoles was stopped by Judge Robinson as he was passing through the courtroom on the way to the street. The judge asked him who wrote the letter signed "Jokester." Mapoles replied that he could not tell him. The judge summoned the city sergeant and ordered him to confine Mapoles to the city jail for thirty days.

The Virginia press reacted sharply to Mapole's fate. The *Richmond Times-Dispatch* wrote:

> The liberty of the press and the right of privileged communication is directly involved. No issue in our courts surpasses this action in importance; there must be a binding determination whether this court, or any court, has the right to upset the principle of such communications.[31]

And the *Richmond News-Leader* editorialized: "If sources of information are not privileged, then freedom of the press is a fiction and political liberty soon will be.[32]

Mapoles petitioned the state supreme court of appeals but was ordered released before the court passed on the petition. He had spent five days in jail.

A year later in Texas, the *Longview News* printed a story alleging that Harrison County officials were permitting transportation of 3.2 beer in exchange for a bribe of ten dollars per load. The district attorney brought the case to the grand jury, and Syril Parker, the editor of the *News*, was ordered to reveal the sources for the article. He refused and was sentenced for contempt.

In Kentucky in 1934 Jack Durham, of the *Danville Advocate*, and Wesley Carty, of the *Louisville Courier-Journal*, received a tip that a hanging in effigy was going to occur in Danville. After waiting at the designated spot for more than an hour, the reporters discovered that Representative J. Sterling Towles had been hanged in effigy for his vote in favor of a state sales tax. The reporters immediately dispatched the story to their respective newspapers and the Associated Press.

Later they were called before a court of inquiry and

asked to name their sources. When they refused, Judge Jay
Harlan ordered them to "think it over" and return in two
days. Again they declined to answer—and were fined. They
were recalled daily, but remained adamant. "We refuse to
answer on the grounds of a newspaper confidence." said
Carty.[33]

Judge Harlan appeared determined to keep the reporters
behind bars if they persisted. "If this is an endurance con-
test," he said, "I can stand it."[34] But Durham and Carty
were also determined not to yield. "No matter how many
times Judge Harlan sends us to jail or how far City Attorney Haguely pushes this case," they said, "we will continue
to uphold what we believe to be one of the highest ideals
of our profession and keep our confidences."[35]

Kentucky newspapers rallied behind the jailed reporters.
"It is a mistake," wrote the *Lexington Leader*, "for anyone
to ask that newspapermen violate their own universally accepted rule of action, which is in the interest of society as
a whole."[36] And the *Courier-Journal* pointed out the ab-
surdity of prosecuting reporters for refusing to reveal
sources on a story about a hanging in effigy:

> Possibly the lyncher of the Court House dummy will
> never be found, though everything has been done save
> the setting of bloodhounds on his trail. It is a sad com-
> mentary that Kentucky has seen actual lynchings that
> drew no such activity on the part of the courts as this
> murder of a ragdoll in Danville.[37]

The incident finally ended when the two men involved
in the "hanging" admitted that they had participated. After
eleven trials, forty-five hours in jail, and twenty-two dollars in fines, Durham and Carty were released.

In 1935 *New York Journal-American* reporter Martin
Mooney wrote a series of articles about the "numbers

racket" gambling operations in New York City, indicating
that they were continuing despite grand-jury investigations.

A New York County grand jury vainly demanded to
know the names of Mooney's informers. Cited for contempt
before the Court of General Sessions, Mooney made the
following statement:

> I cannot answer the questions put to me because I vio-
> late a confidence, and if the day should come when it is
> imperative for me in order to earn my bread and butter
> to double cross people who give me information, off the
> record, then that day, your Honor, I will deem it advis-
> able to tear up this press card.[38]

Judge Morris Koenig found Mooney in contempt, however:

> I know of no law, Mr. Mooney, and none has been
> presented to me so that the Court could consider its judg-
> ment in this State—at least either by the legislature or by
> recognized law—which gives to the witness the privilege
> claimed by him. I said then, as I say now, if a new rule
> of evidence is to be made, either the Legislature of the
> State can do so or the higher courts can lay down a rule
> of evidence.[39]

Mooney was fined $250 and sentenced to thirty days in
jail. He appealed the case, arguing that the principles underlying the privilege extended to lawyers, doctors and priests
should provide the basis for reporters' privilege, and asked
the court to extend the testimonial privilege to journalists.

The New York Court of Appeals was not ready to do
so. It noted that the privilege did not exist in common law,
and that certain states had enacted statutes to establish such
a privilege but New York had not. It weighed the absence
of a statutory privilege heavily in its decision, stating that
if a privilege was to be created, "it should be done by the

Legislature which has thus far refused to enact such legislation."[40]

Mooney was forced to pay the $250 fine and serve thirty days in the Queens County jail.

Four years after Mooney lost his case, a *Toledo* (Ohio) *Times* reporter wrote a story about gambling in his city. The Lucas County grand jury later asked the reporter, Sherman Stambaugh, to inform the grand jury of his sources. Stambaugh would not do so. He was found guilty of contempt of court by Common Pleas Judge James Martin, who dismissed Stambaugh's position as "silly."[41]

In 1940 another gambling revelation appeared in the press. E. B. Chapman wrote an editorial in the *Topeka* (Kansas) *State Journal* about local gambling and liquor conditions. Chapman was summoned by a police court and asked for his sources. In refusing, he observed that the state authorities possessed the information already. Police Judge Peter Caldwell fined him twenty-five dollars for contempt of court.

In 1948 the *New York World-Telegram* published an article charging that widespread gambling and prostitution existed in the city of Newburgh, New York. District Attorney Stanley Johnson claimed that the story was "grossly exaggerated."[42]

In order to convince the people of Newburgh, as well as District Attorney Johnson, that the allegations were factual, the *Newburgh News* carried stories in two subsequent issues that included reproductions of "number slips" circulating in Newburgh.

Johnson subpoenaed *News* reporter Charles Leonard and news editor Douglas Clarke to appear before the grand jury. Both refused to divulge the source for the "number slips" and were sentenced to ten-day jail terms and $100 fines.

Leonard and Clarke issued a statement explaining their position:

The code of ethics of the newspaper profession, without any statutory authority, stipulates without compromise that violation of a confidence is the gravest ethical omission of which a newspaperman may stand accused.

We feel that we are bound to comply with this principle and to make any sacrifice to perpetuate the lofty ideals of the newspaper profession.[43]

In an article written while they were in jail they argued for a legislative privilege:

If a citizen provides valid information to a newspaper, and asks that his name be withheld, honest newspapers go to every extreme to obey that wish.

In our case, we have done just that. We have not betrayed the people. But we have parted company with the law of our state (which is enacted by representatives of those same people).

This enigma can only be resolved by legislation. We knew that long before we were cited for contempt. In accepting punishment for contempt, we were protesting lack of a protective statute in our state.[44]

Leonard and Clarke served five days of their sentence and were freed by a New York State judge on technical grounds. There was no ruling on the existence of a privilege.

In 1960 a woman reporter in Colorado was convicted of contempt for refusing to reveal a news source she used in writing about a former judge who had accepted a bribe. Mrs. Vi Murphy, a reporter for the *Colorado Springs Gazette-Telegraph*, who had obtained advance information on a disciplinary action against the Colorado attorney, claimed a reporters' privilege under the First Amendment. Colorado did not have a privilege statute, and the state Supreme Court sentenced her to thirty days in jail. She attempted to appeal her case to the U.S. Supreme Court, but certiorari was denied[45]—only Justice William Douglas felt the Court should have taken the case. Mrs. Murphy served her full sentence. When she was released, she said she would do the same thing again if necessary.[46]

An unusual case about an allegedly unlawful firing occurred in Hawaii in 1961. In 1957 newsman Alan Goodfader received confidential information that an employee was going to be fired by the Honolulu Civil Service Commission "about a week and a half" before she was actually dismissed.[47]

The employee took her case to court, charging that she had been fired unlawfully. Goodfader was called to testify but would not, on the ground that it would be an abridgment of the First Amendment to disclose where he got his information. "It would be a very grievous breach of my professional ethics for me to say anything which might lead back to my source," he said.[48]

The Supreme Court of Hawaii ruled that Goodfader had to testify. It recognized that "the forced disclosure of a reporter's confidential source of information may, to some extent, constitute an impairment of the freedom of the press,"[49] but could find no precedent for a privilege:

> We readily perceive the disadvantages to a news reporter where his desire to remain silent under a pledge of confidentiality is not accommodated, but we are unable to find, in any of the many decisions touching on the First Amendment that we have been referred to and considered, any basis for concluding that the denial of a claim under the newsman's code constitutes an impairment of Constitutional rights.[50]

The court took special note of the fact that Hawaii did not have any privilege statute:

> In this jurisdiction, no statutory privilege against disclosure is extended to newsmen. Consistently with the

foregoing general rule (that newsmen do not possess a judicial privilege), therefore, no such privilege should be judicially recognized.[51]

Despite the court's ruling, Goodfader never revealed his source or went to jail because he was not called again to testify.

SOCIOLOGICAL CASES

Today a new kind of story is becoming prominent in government/press subpoena controversies. In recent years journalists have used confidential information to write articles about groups and issues not previously covered in the mass media. Investigative reporting on fringe political groups, drug use and abuse, and other issues has provided the public with heretofore unavailable information about the activities of various elements of the society.

Two cases illustrate this new trend.

In 1966 an article about marijuana appeared in the *Daily Emerald*, the University of Oregon student newspaper. Annette Buchanan, the managing editor of the newspaper, had interviewed seven marijuana users for the story, promising them that she would not reveal their identities under any circumstances. The article contained portions of the interviews, but the names were fictitious.

Miss Buchanan's pledge of confidentiality was quickly put to the test as she was subpoenaed by a grand jury and requested to reveal her sources. She was convicted of contempt after the trial court concluded that the privilege she asserted was not a constitutional right and that public policy questions of that nature should be left to the legislature.[52]

She appealed the contempt conviction, arguing that freedom of the press included the freedom to gather news and that certain stories cannot be obtained unless a reporter relies on confidential information. The Oregon Supreme Court rejected her arguments. But it did observe that if the legislature passed a privilege statute, they would be valid: "We hold merely that nothing in the state or Federal Constitution compels the courts, in the absence of a statute, to recognize such a privilege."[53] The U.S. Supreme Court would not hear an appeal,[54] and Miss Buchanan was forced to pay a $300 fine.

The Wisconsin Supreme Court heard a case involving the editor of an underground newspaper who refused to reveal confidential information relating to a bombing in Madison, Wisconsin, in 1970. In *Wisconsin v. Knops*, the court ruled that reporters *did* have a constitutional right to refuse to disclose confidential information, *except* "when such confidence was in conflict with the public's overriding need to know."[55]

In the Knops case the court noted that the source requested was a bombing suspect, weighed the competing interests—the "free flow of information" and the "fair and effective administration of the judicial system"—and chose the latter:

> . . . in a disorderly society such as we are currently experiencing, it may well be appropriate to curtail in a very minor way the free flow of information, if such curtailment will serve the purpose of restoring an atmosphere in which all of our fundamental freedoms can flourish.[56]

The Buchanan and Knops cases set the stage for the three cases heard by the Supreme Court during its 1971 term. All three represented this new type of investigative reporting on societal problems, and all three merit special examination. It was the Court's ruling in these cases that finally resolved the question of whether or not a journalist had a First Amendment right to withhold his sources of information.

5

Pappas, Branzburg and Caldwell: The Landmark Supreme Court Case

IN JULY 1970 Paul Pappas was working as a newsman-photographer for WTEV-TV (Channel 6) in New Bedford, Massachusetts. He had been employed by WTEV for more than seven years, reporting and filming virtually all aspects of the news.

On July 30, 1970, civil disorders erupted in New Bedford. Pappas was in WTEV's Providence, Rhode Island, office when he received a call from Truman Taylor, a newsman in the station's main office. Taylor told Pappas that "they seem to be burning down New Bedford" and asked him to go there to cover a Black Panther news conference and report on the fires and turmoil in the city.

Pappas was given an address on Kempton Street, which turned out to be an abandoned, boarded-up store, purportedly the Black Panther headquarters. When he arrived, the street was barricaded, so he went to WTEV's New Bedford station and informed the news department that he could not get into the store. They asked him to return there, however, because they had received a telephone call indicating that he would be allowed entry.

Pappas returned to the area outside the store and set up a camera on the street. A Panther spokesman named Bob Heard came out of the "headquarters" and read a prepared statement which Pappas photographed and recorded. In the statement Heard indicated that police would be allowed into the Panther headquarters to search for weapons if they had search warrants, if their search was gentlemanly and if they were accompanied by the "news media." Pappas heard a complaint from the Panthers that a police raid would occur and that the news reports would cover only the police side of the story. Pappas replied that the reason the media covered the police was that it "was never allowed to show any other side."

Pappas asked to enter the headquarters. Several Panthers near Heard replied that he could enter only under certain conditions: if a police raid occurred, he would be free to report and photograph what took place, but otherwise anything he saw or heard would be "strictly in confidence." Pappas was guaranteed safe conduct into the headquarters if he returned to the scene. He did return at nine o'clock that evening, accompanied by Rogue Monteiro, an Indian and an employee of WTEV. Monteiro led Pappas through a maze of backyards and alleys and into the headquarters. After about five minutes, Monteiro left.

As soon as Pappas arrived, some of the Panthers demanded to know why he was there, suggesting that he was a "police stoolie." He replied that he was there strictly in his capacity as a reporter and that he had already given his word that he would abide by the established conditions. They asked for his promise again, and he repeated it.

Pappas remained at the headquarters for about three hours. He observed what was going on, talked with the individuals inside the building, but made no notes. A police raid did not occur on that evening, and Pappas kept his promise: he did not write a story about his stay or reveal to anyone what happened while he was there.

Nearly two months later, on September 22, 1970, Pappas was summoned by the Bristol County grand jury. He appeared and answered all questions concerning his name, address, employment, and the things he had seen and heard outside the Panther headquarters. However, he would not answer questions about what he had seen or heard inside: what he had heard the Panthers say inside the headquarters, what the interior looked like, what the names of the occupants were.

On September 24, 1970, Pappas was subpoenaed to appear again before the grand jury on September 28. He filed a motion to quash the subpoena, and his appearance was deferred pending a determination of the motion.

The Superior Court of Bristol County held a hearing on the motion on September 30. Pappas indicated that revealing the information would violate his free speech and free press rights under the First Amendment. He also said that if he breached the confidence ". . . [A]ny future possibilities of obtaining information to be used in my work would be definitely jeopardized, inasmuch as I wouldn't be trusted or couldn't gain anyone's confidence to acquire any information in reporting the news as it is."[1] Furthermore, he said, revealing what he had seen and heard could place him in personal danger.

On October 16, 1970, the Superior Court ruled that "Pappas does not have any privilege and must respond to the subpoena and testify to such questions as may be put to him by the Grand Jury relating to what he saw and heard, and the identity of any persons he may have seen."[2]

The Supreme Judicial Court of Massachusetts affirmed the ruling of the Superior Court on January 29, 1971.[3] The court noted that "Massachusetts, unlike certain other states, has created no statutory privilege protecting news sources"[4] and that to establish a privilege for reporters "would be engaging in judicial amendment of the Constitution or judicial legislation."[5]

Pappas was again subpoenaed to appear before the grand jury on February 5, 1971, but a stay was entered by Justice William Brennan, pending an appeal to the U.S. Supreme Court.

Pappas' argument before the Supreme Court stressed the First Amendment justification for a reporter's privilege. Pappas also stressed that the case "does not involve even the suggestion of a crime committed during the critical period of Pappas' visit to the Panther headquarters."[6] The record was silent on the relationship, "if any, between activities in the Panther headquarters on the night of July 30, 1970, and the Bristol County Grand Jury's investigation. Thus, the Grand Jury inquiry on this record is almost a classic example of a 'fishing expedition.' "[7]

Pappas indicated that a qualified privilege would protect him, and that he did not oppose giving the state an opportunity to demonstrate "both a compelling need for Pappas' appearance before the Grand Jury and an overriding public necessity for his testimony."[8] In determining whether a reporter must testify, Pappas' counsel suggested that the Court establish the following criteria.

The State must demonstrate at the outset that it has reason to believe from non-press sources that a crime has been committed, that the newsman has information relevant to the crime, and that there have been substantial but unsuccessful attempts to obtain this same information elsewhere. This last point is particularly important, because otherwise the reporter's appearance and testimony, despite their adverse effect on First Amendment freedoms, will play only a corroborating role in the Grand Jury's accumulation of evidence. Finally, the State must show the specific purpose for which the newsman's testimony is needed.[9]

The Supreme Court rendered a decision in the case on June 29, 1972. However, because the decision also covered two additional cases, those two cases will be examined before the Court's decision is analyzed.

In October 1969 Paul Branzburg, an investigative reporter for the *Louisville Courier-Journal*, began preparing an article on drug use in Frankfort, Kentucky.

"The process of developing such a story is a complicated and tedious one," said Branzburg. "Information is obtained by moving from contact to contact. This mechanism becomes possible only to the extent that those having information develop trust and confidence in the reporter and develop a feeling of security that their identities will be protected."[10]

In virtually every instance, the first thing discussed with a contact was the confidentiality of his identity. Branzburg showed his contacts a copy of the Kentucky shield statute, which provides:

No person shall be compelled to disclose in any legal proceeding or trial before any court, or before any grand or petit jury, or before the presiding officer of any tribunal, or his agent or agents, or before the General Assembly, or any committee thereof, or before any city or county legislative body, or any committee thereof, or elsewhere, the source of any information procured or obtained by him, and published in a newspaper or by a radio or television broadcasting station by which he is engaged or employed, or with which he is connected.[11]

Sometimes he explained the substance of the statute instead of showing it. In either case, knowing of the statute generally "satisfied the contacts."[12]

One of Branzburg's articles on drug use appeared in the *Courier-Journal* on November 15, 1969. Here is the story Louisville residents read that Saturday morning:

THE HASH THEY MAKE ISN'T TO EAT
by Paul M. Branzburg
Courier-Journal Staff Writer

Larry, a young Louisville hippie, wiped the sweat off his brow, looked about the stuffy little room and put another pot on a stove over which he had been laboring for hours.

For over a week, he has been proudly tending his pots and pans. But he also has paused frequently to peek out the door in search of "The Man" (police).

Larry and his partner, Jack, are engaged in a weird business that is a combination of capitalism, chemistry, and criminality.

They are operating a makeshift laboratory in south-central Louisville that may produce them enough hashish, or "hash", a concentrate of marijuana, to net them up to $5,000 for three weeks of work.

Larry and Jack were once run-of-the-mill dope dealers, but in the past few months they have expanded operations and become dope manufacturers.

On a sunny afternoon last week, Larry entered his "lab" and began another day of cooking hash. With long-handled pruning shears, he began chopping marijuana stems into a large tub.

"I don't know why I'm letting you do this story," he said quietly. "To make the narcs (narcotics detectives) mad, I guess. That's the main reason." However, Larry and his partner asked for and received a promise that their names would be changed.

The room had once been a kitchen, but it now smelled like a stable. A bare lightbulb on the ceiling cast a pallid glow over the cracked pink walls, an old-fashioned gas stove, a green mattress on the floor and a pile of cheap broken furniture in the corner. A filthy sink was stacked with dirty dishes. The floor was covered with discarded marijuana that had already been processed.

'Partly an Ego Trip'

"The trouble we're having is finding the right base," Larry said, as he continued to chop stems. "The hash we've produced gets you stoned, but it doesn't smoke the same way as foreign hash. I tried to use incense as a base, but it gives too much of a sweet taste. In the Middle East they use camel manure, so I'm thinking of going out to the zoo and copping some camel manure."

"For me, making hash is partly an ego trip," he said. "To see how good I can make it. To see how close I can get it to foreign hash. We've gotten it to the right consistency, but not the right taste."

Larry is a tall, slender 21-year-old who has traveled over much of the world and whose parents live in a very comfortable home in the East End. He has been on Louisville's hip scene for about a year.

Jack is a long-haired 20-year-old who has been in Louisville two years. "I came down here when I was 18," he says, "and my sister was turning on, and so I slowly met the hip people."

Have 30 Pounds

Both deny they are manufacturing hash for the money, although they admit that it can be fantastically profitable.

Hashish is most commonly sold at about $7 to $10 per gram, and there are about 29 grams per ounce. Larry and Jack have about 30 pounds of marijuana—originally picked in Kentland, Ind.—and that is enough to yield about five pounds of hashish.

When sold in bulk, hashish brings $800 to $1,000 per pound. Larry and Jack already have five buyers who want a pound apiece. So they should make $4,000 to $5,000 for three weeks of work.

At first glance, it appears that Larry and Jack make a great deal of money. Actually, if they are successful in manufacturing and selling five pounds of hashish, they will probably go out of business for a few months. They have only bothered to make hashish three times this year.

"If you have no status to live up to, you don't worry when you run out of bread (money)," says Jack. "It's nice to work and have nice things, but it's too much of a hassle."

Larry poured rubbing alcohol into the tub of marijuana stems and put it on the stove to cook. Soon the room was full of the sick smell of gaseous alcohol. Larry opened the window and sat down on the mattress to avoid the fumes.

"Actually, this is a service to keep people away from heroin," he said seriously. "Junk is like being dead. You can't eat, sleep or have sex. But hash is enlightening."

The dope duo have divided up business responsibilities. Larry manufactures. Jack is "vice president in charge of sales—or something like that."

Ten days after the article appeared, Branzburg was summoned to appear before the Jefferson County (Kentucky) grand jury. At the grand jury proceeding, he was asked the following questions:

1. On November 12 and 13, 1969, who was the person or persons you observed in possession of marijuana of which you wrote an article in the *Courier-Journal* of November 15, 1969?
2. On November 12 and 13, 1969, who was the person or persons you observed in compounding and mixing marijuana reducing same to a compound known as hashish of which you wrote an

article in the *Courier-Journal* of November 15, 1969?[13]

Branzburg refused to answer, citing the Kentucky shield law.

Jefferson Circuit Court Judge J. Miles Pound heard arguments by Branzburg's lawyer that Branzburg was protected by the state law and by the First Amendment. Judge Pound disagreed and ordered Branzburg to answer the questions in another appearance before the grand jury. Branzburg's attorney filed a petition for relief against Judge Pound, and the Kentucky Court of Appeals granted a temporary order of prohibition pending its review of the case.

On November 27, 1970, the Kentucky Court of Appeals denied Branzburg's petition for relief. The court ruled that "the language of KRS 421.100 [the Kentucky shield statute] granting immunity to a newsman from disclosing the source of any information procured or obtained by him, grants a privilege from disclosing the source of the information but does not grant a privilege against disclosing the information itself."[14] The court ruled that the identity of the persons making hashish was not the source of Branzburg's information, but "the actual source of information in this case was the reporter's personal observation."[15] The court indicated that if an informant had told him of the time and place he could observe individuals making hashish, the identity of that informant would be protected by the statute:

> The reporter, however, was not asked to reveal the identity of any such informant and his privilege from making that disclosure is not in question. He was asked to disclose the identity of persons seen by him in the perpetration of a crime and he refused, urging as a justification for such refusal, that the statute should be given a broad construction extending his privilege against dis-

closure to all his knowledge of this incident rather than just the source of the knowledge.[16]

Chief Judge Edward P. Hill, Jr., dissented. He argued that the court had misconstrued the language and intent of the state statute:

The majority opinion to my mind has adopted a strained and unnecessarily narrow construction of the term "source of any information procured or obtained" used in KRS 421.100. I believe that the phrase "source of any information" is a broad, comprehensive one, certainly not a technical phrase.

The majority opinion stands for the proposition that the statute in question does not apply in instances in which a newspaper reporter witnesses the commission of a crime. But the statute does not place any such limitation on the privilege. It certainly would have been no trouble for the Legislature to have provided for an exception to the privilege had it thought one advisable. The statute in question is the expression of public policy by the proper branch of government, the Legislature, after nearly 150 years' experience, and this court has no business interfering with great and fundamental policy questions of our system of government.

It must be remembered that the present case does not involve injury to life, limb, or property. But even if it did, we have a situation requiring the balance of values, and I believe, as apparently did the Legislature, that the benefits to society from thoroughly and correctly reporting current events greater outweighs the probable and highly imaginary possibility of their abuse under the statute. Who ever heard of a man about to commit a crime against life, limb, or property either calling in a newspaper reporter or soliciting a newspaper reporter to witness the crime upon being assured that the reporter would not disclose what he was about to observe? Actually, the privilege provided in the statute is one which the newspaper people may weigh, and I have greater confidence in the newspaper world than to think it would participate in such an imaginary scheme or refuse to divulge important information obtained under such circumstances.[17]

Branzburg filed a motion to reconsider on December 7, 1970. With the case still pending, he continued his work as a reporter. On Sunday morning, January 10, 1971, two of his pieces appeared in the *Courier-Journal*: one was a "news analysis" entitled "Pot Problem Byproduct: Disrespect for the Law;" the other was an article headlined "Rope Turns to Pot." Both dealt with drug use in Franklin County. As a result, Branzburg was subpoenaed to appear on January 18 before the Franklin County grand jury. Branzburg moved to quash the subpoena before Franklin Circuit Court Judge Henry Meigs, but the motion was denied.

On January 22, 1971, the Court of Appeals rendered a further ruling in Branzburg's first case, denying the motion to reconsider. The court also denied Branzburg's appeal in the Meigs case.

Branzburg petitioned the U. S. Supreme Court for a writ of certiorari. The Court agreed to hear his appeal.

Branzburg argued before the Court that a First Amendment privilege should be declared:

> Consistent with the First Amendment rights demonstrated above, this Court should unhesitatingly declare that there exists a privilege under the First Amendment against compulsory appearances of reporters in closed proceedings and compulsory disclosure from reporters of confidential information. The privilege should state that absent a prior showing in an open hearing of a compelling and overriding need by the government for the

information sought, freedom of the press under the First Amendment precludes such compulsion against the reporter.[18]

The Court also heard the case of Paul Pappas and the case of the reporter discussed next, Earl Caldwell.

Earl Caldwell, a black reporter for the *New York Times*, had been assigned to the *Times'* San Francisco office "after the resident correspondents in San Francisco, Wallace Turner and Lawrence Davies, found that they could not effectively report on the activities" of the Black Panthers and other dissident groups.[19]

Caldwell's experience as a reporter had enabled him to develop contacts throughout the black community. Yet his ability to cover militant groups did not come easily. He explained his background in a recent magazine article:

I was on the balcony with Martin Luther King in 1968, and I saw him die. I saw the blood come out of his neck and stack up around his head. I watched Ralph Abernathy cradle King's head in his arms. I was there, and I looked into King's eyes and watched him die.

Before that I had done my time in the streets. I wasn't just in Newark or Detroit. I was on Blue Hill Avenue in Boston. I was on the west side in Dayton. I was in Cincinnati and Watts and Sacramento and Chicago and a lot of other places where black folks showed their anger and rebelled during the summer of 1967.

I remember being in Newark and visiting a young kid in his home just after his mother had been fatally shot. There were twelve in that family, and their father was dead. Their mother had locked them inside the apartment when the rioting broke out, and she was lying on a couch. She got up—maybe to get a drink of water or maybe to see about the food on the stove. It makes no difference. The thing that's worth remembering is that when she got up a bullet came through a window and tore her neck apart. When I arrived, with my press card, there was only a pool of blood left and holes in the walls that were bigger than your first. The next morning the stories in my paper were not about police and National Guardsmen firing weapons so powerful that they dug walls apart. The *Times* headlined stories about snipers— snipers who the governor of New Jersey said were operating in the black community and who were highly professional (in spite of the fact that they never killed anyone).

Out of that summer came Rap Brown. I went across the country with him, and I watched thousands of black folks who were fed up, who were so filled with rage that they, too, were about to explode. Out of all that came the Black Panther party.[20]

Despite this background, Caldwell did not gain the complete confidence of the Panthers for a number of months. "I found that in those first months they were very brief and reluctant to discuss any substantive matter with me."[21] The Panthers called him a cop. "I had to be a cop, they reasoned: the *New York Times* was not about to send a black reporter 3,000 miles just to cover them."[22]

However, as time passed, Caldwell became accepted as a journalist. As Caldwell observed:

I had friends who knew Kathleen Cleaver; she was my first contact with the party. But to make it, you had to be able to deal with the Panthers in the streets, the Panthers whose names you never asked, whose names you never read in the paper. They were the ones who showed me what I needed to know. Late one night in San Francisco they yanked an old couch away from a wall in a cramped apartment, exposing stacks of guns of every sort. I could tell my readers then to take these people seriously, and I did.

I watched the Panthers' breakfast program before

other reporters knew it existed. I wrote about it in the *Times*. If I've ever written a page-one story, that was it. The story was all there, but it was buried somewhere in the thickness of the Sunday edition. I told how painstakingly they went about their work, cooking big breakfasts —eggs, bacon, ham, grits, biscuits—they had it all. But they also added politics, in the songs they sang, in the literature they gave to the kids. Nobody tried to hide the political part from me—the reporter from the *New York Times*. Every now and then I'd get the third degree. "C'mon now, Caldwell: we know you're a cop," they'd say. But I kept coming back, and I kept telling them: "I'm a reporter. That's my job. That's the only reason— the only reason I'm here." Somewhere along the line they began to believe me.

As I became more deeply involved with the Panthers, I began to keep all kinds of files on them. On Panther personalities. On off-the-record conversations. I kept tapes, too, and I would write my personal reactions to everything involving the Panthers that I covered. At this point they were under attack by police groups across the country. At a time when the party was shutting out reporters, I was closer to it than ever. I would sit nights at the national headquarters on Shattuck Avenue in Berkeley, talking with anyone who would talk. Often I would not leave until 3 or 4 in the morning. The party trusted me so much that I did not have to ask for permission to bring along a tape recorder.[23]

Caldwell's confidential relationship with the Panthers enabled him to write stories that no one else in the country could have written. The articles informed readers of the *New York Times*—as well as readers of as many as sixty other newspapers—about the Black Panther Party and made an enormous contribution to public understanding of a previously unknown phenomenon.

In late 1969, according to Caldwell, the FBI "began to

interfere with my work. They wanted to pick my brain. They wanted me to slip about behind my news sources, to act like the double agents I saw on old movie reruns on TV."[24] The FBI began calling Caldwell on a daily basis. *Time*s bureau chief Wallace Turner had an assistant in the bureau, Alma Brackett, take all of Caldwell's calls, but they still kept coming. Between December 23, 1969, and January 12, 1970, FBI agents attempted six times to interview Caldwell, but he refused to see them. Then one day an agent told Mrs. Brackett that if Caldwell didn't come in and talk to them, he'd be telling what he knew in court.

On February 2, 1970, Caldwell was served with a subpoena to appear before a federal grand jury in San Francisco. His attorneys informed the government that they intended to quash the subpoena. The government decided to continue the subpoena indefinitely and to issue another on March 16.

Caldwell's lawyers contacted government counsel Victor Woerheide and indicated that it was important to know the subject of the inquiry to determine if information sought from Caldwell was at all relevant. Woerheide said that the subject of the investigation was "no concern of a witness" and that he could not define it further.[25]

On March 17 Caldwell and the *New York Times* made a motion to the U.S. District Court for the Northern District of California to quash the subpoenas on the grounds that freedom of the press should not be jeopardized in the absence of an overriding governmental interest; the subpoenas intruded on confidential associations necessary for the effective exercise of First Amendment rights; the subpoenas were based on information obtained by electronic surveillance, which violated Caldwell's Fourth Amendment rights.

The motion was heard by Judge Alfonso Zirpoli on

April 3, 1970, at which time the government withdrew the
February 2 subpoena. Judge Zirpoli denied the motion,
but he did issue a protective order limiting the scope of
Caldwell's questioning by the grand jury:

> . . . he need not reveal confidential associations that
> impinge upon the effective exercise of his First Amend-
> ment right to gather news for dissemination to the public
> through the press or other recognized media until such
> time as a compelling and overriding national interest
> which cannot be alternatively served has been estab-
> lished to the satisfaction of the Court.[26]

Judge Zirpoli stayed the effective date of his decision,
pending appeal, and on April 17 Caldwell appealed to the
Ninth Circuit Court of Appeals. On May 12 the Court of
Appeals dismissed the appeal without opinion.

Meanwhile the term of the grand jury that had issued the
March 16 subpoena expired, and a new grand jury was
sworn in. A new subpoena was issued on May 22, which
Caldwell and the *Times* moved to quash on the same
grounds as the earlier one. Judge Zirpoli again denied the
motion and on June 4 issued a protective order substan-
tially the same as that of April 8. On the same day Caldwell
refused to appear before the grand jury. The next day, in
District Court, he repeated his refusal. He was held in contempt, but the court stayed its contempt order pending
appeal.

On November 16 the Ninth Circuit Court of Appeals
ruled that the District Court protective order was not sufficient to cover the First Amendment interests involved, and
that Caldwell did not have to appear before the grand jury
until the government could demonstrate an overriding interest and lack of an alternative source.

The court observed:

If the Grand Jury may require appellant to make available to it information obtained by him in his capacity as news gatherer, then the Grand Jury and the Department of Justice have the power to appropriate appellant's investigative efforts to their own behalf—to convert him after the fact into an investigative agent of the Government. The very concept of a free press requires that the news media be accorded a measure of autonomy; that they should be free to pursue their own investigations to their own ends without fear of governmental interference; and that they should be able to protect their investigative processes. To convert news gatherers into Department of Justice investigators is to invade the autonomy of the press by imposing a governmental function upon them. To do so where the result is to diminish their future capacity as news gatherers is destructive of their public function. To accomplish this where it has not been shown to be essential to the Grand Jury inquiry simply cannot be justified in the public interest.

The court emphasized, however, that "the rule of this case is a narrow one. It is not every news source that is as sensitive as the Black Panther Party has been shown to be respecting the performance of the 'establishment' press or the extent to which that performance is open to view. It is not every reporter who so uniquely enjoys the trust and confidence of his sensitive news sources."[28]

In a concurring opinion, Judge Jameson stated that Caldwell "did not have any express constitutional right to decline to appear before the grand jury. This is a duty required of all citizens. Nor has Congress enacted legislation to accord any type of privilege to a news reporter."[29] Judge Jameson felt the order of the District Court could have been affirmed, but he agreed with the Court of Appeals' opinion because it achieved the same result and avoided "any unnecessary impingement of First Amendment rights."[30]

The government appealed the case to the U.S. Supreme Court, and the Court ruled on it in conjunction with the Pappas and Branzburg cases.

Caldwell argued before the Court that the Court of Appeals decision should be upheld, and that the First Amendment should enable reporters, in the absence of compelling need, to protect their sources:

> A cardinal aim of the First Amendment is to assure the public dissemination of information necessary to educate a self-governing people concerning the significant issues of the times. The Court of Appeals properly found as a fact that this interest is vitally impaired by the compulsion of newsmen's testimony in a manner which, by jeopardizing their confidential relations with their news sources, chokes off this information at the root. It properly held as a matter of law that this sort of drastic harm to First Amendment interests requires some accommodation of the competing interests of grand jury investigation. The balance struck by the Court of Appeals between these interests forbids the compulsion of a newsman's testimony concerning confidential information in the absence of a compelling showing of investigative need.[31]

On June 29, 1972, the Supreme Court finally resolved the question that had remained unsettled for fourteen years. It ruled that journalists do *not* have a First Amendment right to withhold confidential sources or information from a grand jury. Five justices joined in the majority and four dissented. Justice Byron White, author of the majority opinion, wrote:

> Fair and effective law enforcement aimed at providing security for the person and property of the individual is a fundamental function of government, and the grand jury

plays an important, constitutionally mandated role in this process. On the records now before us, we perceive no basis for holding that the public interest in law enforcement and in ensuring effective grand jury proceedings is insufficient to override the consequential, but uncertain, burden on news gathering which is said to result from insisting that reporters, like other citizens, respond to relevant questions put to them in the course of a valid grand jury investigation or criminal trial.

In my opinion, the majority's reasoning process was weak in three respects.

First, the undue emphasis on combating crime suggests that they "missed the forest for the trees." Justice White said that the Court "cannot seriously entertain the notion that the First Amendment protects a newsman's agreement to conceal the criminal conduct of his source, or evidence thereof, on the theory that it is better to write about crime than to do something about it." Justice White has artificially limited the alternatives. Writing about crime and doing something about it are not mutually exclusive. In fact, if reporters' sources are protected, more instances of crime and corruption will be reported and hence come to the attention of law-enforcement officers. The government should be able to combat crime without relying on reporters to do its detective work. In fact, attorneys general in states that have privilege statutes for reporters indicate that such laws have *not* hindered the battle against crime.[32]

In short, the concern about crime which pervades the majority opinion is misplaced in a discussion of the First Amendment rights of the people to receive a free flow of news.

Second, the majority opinion places too much emphasis on the historical rationale for grand juries, that of "protecting citizens against unfounded criminal prosecutions." Such platitudes cannot obscure the reality in 1973—that grand juries today are tools of the prosecutor.[33] As Justice Potter Stewart noted in his dissent, grand juries are "in effect, immune from judicial supervision" and can be convened by prosecutors "with no serious law-enforcement purpose." In other words, grand juries can be employed by prosecutors to harass and intimidate the press: their investigative powers are broad and unchecked. Thus, in buttressing an institution that serves a questionable purpose, the Court claims that it is strengthening law-enforcement efforts.

Third, although the majority opinion concedes that "[T]he argument that the flow of news will be diminished by compelling reporters to aid the grand jury in a criminal investigation is not irrational," it nevertheless casually dismisses the argument. The Court observes that there is no concrete proof that sources will "dry up" as a consequence. It also argues that "[F]rom the beginning of our country the press has operated without constitutional protection for press informants, and the press has flourished."

The problem with such an argument is threefold.

First, until recently, there has been a de facto recognition of a privilege. The case of former New York Republican Governor Thomas E. Dewey is illustrative:

> The governor has had ten years experience as a prosecutor of crime. In all his experience he has never found it necessary or desirable to attempt to compel any newspaperman to reveal the source of his information. He has a deep understanding of problems of the men of the press and the need to protect the sources of information.[34]

The press has never before operated in a period when it was besieged by as many subpoenas as in recent years.

Second, even granting that a privilege has not heretofore existed, there is no way to measure accurately whether the press has "flourished." In comparison to what? How can we know if the press would not have "flourished" to a significantly greater extent if its sources had been constitutionally protected?

Third—and most important—while a curtailment of the free flow of information cannot be measured with scientific precision, there is substantial evidence of its existence (and that evidence will be examined in succeeding chapters). As Justice Stewart put it in his dissent:

> But we have never before demanded that First Amendment rights rest on elaborate empirical studies demonstrating beyond any conceivable doubt that deterrent effects exist; we have never before required proof of the exact number of people potentially affected by governmental action, who would actually be dissuaded from engaging in First Amendment activity.

Justice Powell's concurring opinion, which Justice Stewart understandably termed "enigmatic," attempts to ameliorate the harshness of the majority opinion by suggesting that "we do not hold, as suggested in the dissenting opinion, that state and federal authorities are free to 'annex' the news media as 'an investigative arm of government.'" It would be hard to argue, however, that that is not precisely what was sanctioned in the cases of Pappas, Branzburg and Caldwell.

Justice Stewart's dissent (joined by Justices Brennan and Marshall) indicts the majority for taking a "crabbed view of the First Amendment" which "reflects a disturbing insensitivity to the critical role of an independent press in our society."

The dissent emphasized the important role of confidential information and explained why confidences were so often necessary:

An officeholder may fear his superior; a member of the bureaucracy, his associates; a dissident, the scorn of majority opinion. All may have information valuable to the public discourse, yet each may be willing to relate that information only in confidence to a reporter whom he trusts, either because of excessive caution or because of a reasonable fear of reprisals or censure for unorthodox views. After today's decision, the potential informant can never be sure that his identity or off-the-record communications will not subsequently be revealed through the compelled testimony of a newsman.

Justice Stewart declared that a First Amendment privilege *should* exist and that when a reporter is subpoenaed the government must "(1) show that there is probable cause to believe that the newsman has information which is clearly relevant to a specific probable violation of law; (2) demonstrate that the information sought cannot be obtained by alternative means less destructive of First Amendment rights; and (3) demonstrate a compelling and overriding interest in the information," before the privilege can be divested.

Justice Douglas authored a separate dissent in which he declared his view that the First Amendment granted journalists an absolute privilege. "Sooner or later," he indicated, "any test which provides less than blanket protection to beliefs and associations will be twisted and relaxed so as to provide virtually no protection at all." Justice Douglas also warned that the decision would "impede the wide open and robust dissemination of ideas and counterthought" necessary in a free society:

The intrusion of government into this domain is symptomatic of the disease of this society. As the years pass the power of government becomes more and more pervasive. It is a power to suffocate both people and causes. Those in power, whatever their politics, want only to perpetuate it. Now that the fences of the law and the tradition that has protected the press are broken down, the people are the victims. The First Amendment, as I read it, was designed precisely to prevent that tragedy.

Several months after the Court's ruling, Earl Caldwell's observations tended to substantiate Justice Stewart's and Justice Douglas' fears. The effect of the Court's decision was not indirect or theoretical:

> I ripped up the notebooks. I erased the tapes and shredded almost every document that I had that dealt with the Panthers. Many of those items should have been saved, for history's sake, as much as for anything. But in America today a reporter cannot save his notes or his tapes or other documents.
>
> That's not all. From now on no newspaper can hope to cover effectively an organization such as the Panthers. I don't care how black a reporter is, he won't get close. He won't, and he shouldn't try. He won't because he cannot be trusted as a reporter. When he goes out and cuts an interview, he may say that it's only for his paper. He may swear to it. But if he means it, the government can now put him in jail and keep him there. Ask me. I know. I was the test case.[35]

Neither Caldwell nor Pappas had to go to jail as a result of the decision because the grand juries that had subpoenaed them had terminated. The consequences of the decision for Branzburg were more immediate: he faced a sentence of six months in jail. Instead of going to jail, however, he decided to go to Michigan. He is currently working as a reporter for the *Detroit Free Press*, and he says that he will not return voluntarily to Kentucky to serve out a sentence he believes is unjust.

Kentucky officials are attempting to extradite Branzburg, and in January 1973 the extradition papers were on the desk of Michigan Governor Milliken.

6

Post-Branzburg Cases:
The Pressure Intensifies

THERE HAVE BEEN a great number of cases since the
Supreme Court's landmark decision, five of which have
already been examined: the *Columbia State*, the *Los
Angeles Times* in the Watergate case, station KFWB in
Los Angeles, Joe Weiler of the *Memphis Commerical Appeal*, and William Farr of the *Los Angeles Herald-Examiner*. Others also merit special notice.

In early 1972 the general manager for WBAI-FM radio
in New York City, Edwin Goodman, was asked to provide
the Manhattan district attorney's office with thirty hours of
tapes broadcast on WBAI during a prisoner insurrection in
1970 at the Manhattan Men's House of Detention, better
known as the Tombs.

Goodman refused. Although New York has a state

shield law, it did not cover material that had been broadcast. Goodman argued that the state law should apply
because of the "transitory, perishable quality" of a broadcast, noting that "if the information were truly a matter of
public record the District Attorney would not need to obtain it by subpoena."[1]

The tapes contained interviews with prisoners who
wanted to remain anonymous. Goodman claimed that
"[t]his significant medium for the direct interchange of
thought would be frozen out of existence were each caller
to realize that the thought from the top of his head, the
possible burst of inspiration or embarrassing error would
find its way into the files of the prosecutor."[2] This did not
convince State Supreme Court Justice Gerald Culkin.
Goodman was convicted of contempt and sentenced to
thirty days in jail. In addition, the station was fined $250.

After spending forty-four hours behind bars, Goodman
was released and cleared of the charges after the district
attorney's office asked the court to "forget about" the case.
The district attorney had become convinced that the tapes
no longer existed, and the court's appellate division reluc-
tantly agreed to drop the charges.[3]

The first reporter to be jailed after the Branzburg decision was Peter Bridge, who covered City Hall for the
now-defunct *Newark Evening News*. Bridge spent three
weeks in jail for refusing to reveal his sources for a story
which appeared on the front page of the paper on May 2,
1972. It began:

> Mrs. Pearl Beatty, a commissioner of the Newark Hous-
> ing Authority, said yesterday an unknown man offered
> to pay her $10,000 to influence her vote for the appoint-
> ment of an executive director of the Authority.
>
> Mrs. Beatty said also that at least two other commis-
> sioners had been harassed and threatened in efforts to
> control their votes.

The charges by Mrs. Beatty, who is also secretary of the city's Insurance Fund Commission, follow a statement by Mayor Kenneth A. Gibson that he "suspects that the attempt to force the selection of an executive director is being manipulated by organized criminal elements in the Newark area."

The mayor's statement, like Mrs. Beatty's, contained no names, and both refused to elaborate. Mrs. Beatty said "a man walked into my office and offered me $10,000 if I would vote for 'their' choice for executive director."

She added, however, that she did not know the man, and probably would not recognize him if she saw him again. "But we've taken everything we have to (U.S. Attorney Herbert J.) Stern." . . .

After the story appeared, a special grand jury was convened by the Essex County prosecutor. Bridge was subpoenaed to appear, and his efforts to quash the subpoena were unsuccessful. Bridge came before the grand jury and answered questions about material in his story. He refused to answer five questions about unpublished information he had received:

—Mr. Bridge, would you please tell us whether Mrs. Beatty provided a description of the unknown man?
—Did Mrs. Beatty provide you with specific acts of harassment and threats other than those outlined in the newspaper article?
—Within the framework of this: "A man enters into my office and offers me $10,000 if I would vote for their choice for executive director" did Mrs. Beatty indicate who their choice for executive director was?
—Mr. Bridge, in addition to that which is contained in the article, what else did Mrs. Beatty say? Did she say it was a tall man, a white man, a black man, a heavy man, a short man?

—Mr. Bridge, did Mrs. Beatty indicate when, in fact, the bribe offer took place?[4]

At the contempt hearing Bridge argued that the First Amendment gave him a privilege on behalf of the public to withhold information sought by the grand jury. Bridge also invoked the New Jersey shield statute, which provides:

> Subject to Rule 37, a person engaged on, connected with, or employed by, a newspaper has a privilege to refuse to disclose the source, author, means, agency or person from or through whom any information published in such newspaper was procured, obtained, supplied, furnished, or delivered.[5]

Rule 37 provides that a person "waives his right or privilege to refuse to disclose . . . a specified matter if he . . . without coercion and with knowledge of his right or privilege, made disclosure of any part of the privileged matter."[6]

Superior Court Judge H. Curtis Meanor dismissed the First Amendment argument on the basis of the Branzburg decision and ruled that Bridge was not covered by the New Jersey statute either:

> In my judgment, by identifying Mrs. Beatty as the source of the information about the bribe offer and about the harassment and threats to other commissioners, Mr. Bridge waived his newspaperman's privilege otherwise provided by the statute, as to anything he obtained from Mrs. Beatty at any time up to the publication of this article concerning or relevant to, i.e., the bribe offered to her of $10,000 and the harassing and threatening of other commissioners. Anything he obtained about those subject matters thereafter which has not been published, of course, there is no waiver.[7]

Ironically, because of Rule 37, Bridge forfeited his immunity by naming his source in the article. If he had not named Mrs. Beatty, he could have successfully shielded his information from grand jury subpoena!

On September 12 the Superior Court of New Jersey, Appellate Division, affirmed Judge Meanor's decision that Bridge had to testify and answer the questions.

The Supreme Court of New Jersey declined to hear the case on September 26, but the sentence of contempt was stayed until October 3 to allow the U.S. Supreme Court to act on a motion for stay.

The high court considered the stay on October 3, and with Justice Douglas dissenting, denied it. On October 4 Bridge went to jail.

Bridge spent three weeks in the Essex County Jail and was finally released when the grand jury disbanded and released its report. That report did not contain indictments, but it was critical of the mayor of Newark and Mrs. Beatty for making statements to the press about crime in city government.

Bridge was free, since his imprisonment could last only as long as the grand jury remained impaneled. However, in January 1973 the Supreme Court was still considering Bridge's petition for a writ of certiorari in his case. The appeal concerned the issue of whether a prosecutor should "be allowed the unrestricted use of a reporter's testimony to criticize a public official by way of grand jury report."[8] It appeared extremely unlikely that the Supreme Court would agree to hear the case.

A number of other cases were also pending appeal in early 1973.

One of them began in July 1971 when the editors of the *Baltimore Evening Sun* assigned reporter David Lightman to investigate the activities of young people at Ocean City, Maryland. The first Lightman story, "Teens Play at Panhandling," appeared on July 20, to be followed six days later by two more, "New Religions Appear on Boardwalk" and "Ocean City: Where the Drugs Are?"

The third article described an incident in a pipe shop at the end of the Ocean City boardwalk:

> A shop near the lower end of the boardwalk wants to be sure its customers are satisfied with the pipes they buy. So salesmen sometimes let them draw some marijuana before they make a purchase.
>
> The shop has pipes for all purposes—combination pipes, with bowls for opium, tea, and hash; adjustable pipes for smoking pot with and without water; buckle pipes, which clip on to one's belt buckle (and are thus easily camouflaged), and others.
>
> Last Friday night, a uniformed Ocean City policeman was standing in another part of the shop. The shopkeeper, her legs stretched out on a waterbed in the next room, tried to explain uses of the various pipes to a customer.
>
> The shopkeeper asked him if he would like to "draw some grass." He pointed to the officer.
>
> "Don't worry about him. We have a lot of cops come in. You know, it's rough for them, most are under 21. We're nice to 'em, so they don't come sniffing around." The customer declined the offer.[9]

On August 9 Lightman was summoned before the Worcester County grand jury to testify concerning his knowledge of suspected illegal drug traffic in Ocean City, Maryland.

The grand jury asked him to state the location of the pipe shop referred to in his article and to give a description of the shopkeeper. Lightman refused, claiming that the shopkeeper was the source of his article. (The Maryland shield statute protects reporters from being compelled to disclose in any legal proceeding "the source of any news or information procured or obtained by him for and published in the newspaper."[10])

The state's attorney instituted contempt proceedings, and the Circuit Court for Worcester County found Lightman guilty of civil contempt. The court noted that there was no testimony that Lightman had identified himself to the shopkeeper as a newspaper reporter and that she had given him information based upon the representation or knowledge that he was a newsman. The court therefore concluded that Lightman was a stranger to the shopkeeper, that what he heard was not conveyed in confidence and that the shopkeeper was not a "source" of information for the article within the meaning of the Maryland statute. The court also rejected Lightman's arguments that his First Amendment rights were violated by being compelled to reveal his source.

On August 4, 1972, the Maryland Court of Special Appeals ruled in the case and interpreted the state shield law. The court observed that the Maryland statute "does not protect against the disclosure of communications; it privileges only the source of the information . . ."[11] However, it recognized that the statute was broad enough "to encompass any source of news or information, without regard to whether the source gave his information in confidence or not. Consequently, it is for the newsman to determine whether he will disclose the 'source' of his news or information, and such disclosure cannot be compelled by requiring that he answer questions aimed, directly or indirectly, toward ascertaining the source's identity."[12]

However, the court went on to indicate that in the Lightman case the shopkeeper was not a source:

> Where a newsman, by dint of his own investigative efforts, personally observes conduct constituting the commission of criminal activities by persons at a partic-

ular location, the newsman, and not the persons observed, is the "source" of the news or information in the
sense contemplated by the statute.[13]

The court suggested that if the testimonial privilege was
to be broadened to extend beyond the source to the information itself, "it can only be done by the Legislature."[14]

The decision was affirmed by the Maryland Court of
Appeals, the state's highest court, on October 17. Lightman was sentenced to thirty days in jail, but the case is
currently pending appeal to the U.S. Supreme Court.

Another case not yet resolved arose out of the Attica
Prison riots in 1971. Between September 9 and September
13, of that year, prisoners at the New York State Correctional Facility at Attica took control of the prison and held
about thirty-eight correctional officers and civilians as hostages. WGR-TV (Buffalo) television reporter Stewart Dan
and cameramen Roland Barnes, Jay LaMarsh and Terry
Johnson covered the riot.

On September 9 the prisoners asked that a TV camera
crew be sent into the prison. Cameraman Johnson and
reporter Dan went inside Attica, shot film and made notes.
WGR-TV broadcast a half-hour news special that evening,
using Johnson's film with narration by Dan. On September
10 Dan and cameramen Barnes and LaMarsh took films
and interviews inside the prison. Some of the exclusive foot-
age was made available to the major television networks.
The WGR-TV reporters and cameramen entered the prison
during the next three days, and their efforts provided
photographs for *Newsweek*, *Time* and *Life*.

On September 13 the prison was besieged by police and
correctional officers, and the state regained control. Forty-
three inmates and hostages were killed during the police
assault. There were no WGR-TV reporters inside the
prison during the attack.

A Wyoming County (New York) special grand jury was convened later to inquire into possible criminal acts by inmates during the riot. The state attorney general served four subpoenas on WGR-TV and its employees.

The first subpoena was handed to news director Sid Hayman. It required "all video tapes and other photographic material in your custody and control which was publicly aired over channel 2 WGR at any time relating to the events at and in the Attica correctional facility between September 9, 1971, to September 13, 1971."[15] WGR-TV stated its intention to comply with the subpoena, since the station felt there was no privilege for publicly broadcast films and tapes. Although a member of the attorney general's staff viewed the films, they were never shown to the grand jury.

The other subpoenas, served on Dan, Barnes and La-Marsh, directed them to testify before the grand jury on April 26, 1972. LaMarsh's appearance was postponed pending a determination of the issues presented by Dan and Barnes.

Dan and Barnes read the following statement, which they referred to when asked to answer questions about occurrences inside the prison while they were reporting and filming there:

> I entered Attica Penitentiary between September 9 and September 13, 1971 in the course of my employment as a newscaster. My sole and only purpose for being there was to gather and disseminate news to the general public. Therefore, as to those matters which occurred inside of the prison during those days, I respectfully decline to answer any questions. I do so as a protected newscaster and professional journalist within the provisions of Section 79-h of the Civil Rights Law and in furtherance of the First Amendment Constitutional right

of freedom of the press and in furtherance of the public's interest in free and untrammeled news reporting.[16]

State Supreme Court Judge Carmen Ball cited the Supreme Court's decision in the Branzburg case in denying the constitutional claim. He also ruled that the New York statute did not apply, since the reporters failed to demonstrate that the withheld information was based on confidential communications or sources.

On January 9, 1973, the case was appealed before the appellate division of the state Supreme Court. Dan and Barnes argued that the state statute did not refer to "confidential" information but protected *all* news and information. A decision had not yet been rendered in the case as of February 1, 1973.

A misdemeanor was the focal point of a subpoena controversy in Delaware in late 1972. On September 23 a busing demonstration took place at Mount Pleasant High School in Wilmington. Ronald Dubick, a *Wilmington News-Journal* photographer, witnessed the event and took photographs for the newspapers.

Four days later, Charles McGowan, the director of photography at the *News-Journal*, was served with a subpoena signed by the chief deputy attorney general of Delaware. He was directed to present pictures taken by Dubick at the demonstration to Sergeant Clark Jester, a state policeman.

Sergeant Jester wanted the photographs to attempt to identify a demonstrator who allegedly made obscene remarks to him on September 23. Jester did not know who made the remarks, but he thought the photographs might enable another member of the police department to identify the person.

McGowan moved to quash the subpoena but the Superior Court denied his motion on November 1, 1972. McGowan appealed the case to the Supreme Court of

Delaware, where his attorney, Rodman Ward, argued that the subpoena should have been quashed:

> Several facts stand out in this effort to subpoena the press.
>
> First, the offense thought to have occurred is a misdemeanor of the mildest kind. [The maximum punishment is a $10 fine and ten days in jail.]
>
> Second, there is no present suspect.
>
> Third, the policeman in question cannot identify the offender but thinks his fellow policeman "might" be able to.
>
> Fourth, the entire matter is a police concern. The Attorney General, at the request of the police, provided legal advice as to what offense might have been committed and issued a subpoena when asked to.
>
> This is, then, a case where the police seek to annex the news media as an investigatory arm in a police inquiry into and offense of the most petty sort. The newsphotographer becomes, by his coverage of a news story of public interest, the investigating reporter for the police.[17]

As of the end of January 1973 the Delaware Supreme Court had not rendered a decision.

A Tennessee television personality found himself involved in a subpoena controversy in November 1972. Harry Thornton, host of the *Morning Show* on WDEF-TV (Chattanooga), received a call from a person who identified himself as a "member of the grand jury" investigating former city judge Bennie Harris. The caller said that the case had been "whitewashed."

Thornton aired the comments live. "I did not relay anything," Thornton said, "He called me and spoke directly to the audience on the air."[18]

Thornton was asked to name the caller before the county grand jury. He refused, saying that to do so would be "a blow to the freedom of the press."[19]

Hamilton County Criminal Court Judge Tillman Grand found Thornton guilty of contempt and sent him to jail. On December 20 he was released, pending a hearing before the state Supreme Court in Knoxville. A hearing was held on January 11, but no decision had been rendered by the end of the month.

As this book went to press, eleven reporters and officials of *Time*, the *New York Times*, the *Washington Star-News* and the *Washington Post* were subpoenaed by Republican attorneys in civil suits arising from the Watergate bugging incident.

The cases that have been discussed—both recent ones and early ones—are only the tip of the iceberg; they do not accurately portray the extent of the subpoena problem. For example, between January 1969 and July 1971, CBS and NBC television networks received 124 subpoenas for reporters' notes or film.[20] In the same period, the *Chicago Sun-Times* and *Chicago Daily News* received a total of thirty subpoenas, two thirds of them on behalf of the government.[21] The *Los Angeles Times* has "fought thirty subpoenas involving either our people or our information" in the past four years.[22]

The magnitude of the problem cannot be disputed. Nor can the fact be denied that reporters must now seriously consider the prospect of going to jail. But how are the American people affected? Is this problem of concern to anyone outside the journalistic community? What are the consequences for the average citizen if the law continues to demand that reporters turn over their notes and sources? These questions will be taken up in the next chapters.

PART III

THE
ARGUMENTS

7

Why Subpoenas Threaten the Right to Know

THE BASIC RATIONALE for the establishment of a newsman's privilege is not particularly complex. Four premises form the basis for the "free flow of information" argument.

First, a free press is the very foundation of our democratic institutions.

Second, a free press should be given "the broadest scope that can be countenanced in an orderly society."

Third, information received from confidential sources is an integral part of modern news-gathering operations.

Fourth, without a legal privilege for journalists, public access to valuable information is imperiled.

A free press is the very foundation of our democratic institutions. The most reliable indicator in determining whether a society strives to be free or totalitarian is the extent to which the press is free—free to investigate, to criticize, to publish whatever it deems fit to publish.

It is instructive to recall the attitudes regarding freedom of the press of two powerful leaders in contemporary history. Adolph Hitler once said:

> The organization of our press has truly been a success. Our law concerning the press is such that divergencies of opinion between members of the government are no longer an occasion for public exhibitions, which are not the newspapers' business. We've eliminated that conception of political freedom which holds that everybody has the right to say whatever comes into his head.[1]

Or consider the words of Nikolai Lenin:

> Why should freedom of speech and freedom of the press be allowed? Why should a government which is doing what it believes to be right allow itself to be criticized? It would not allow opposition by lethal weapons. Ideas are much more fatal things than guns. Why should any man be allowed to buy a printing press and disseminate pernicious opinion calculated to embarrass the government?[2]

There is no doubt that the society with a free, unregulated press—despite its defects—will be the freest, most desirable society in which to live. Perhaps James Madison most eloquently expressed the view that if a society is going to strive to be democratic, its press must be free:

> Nothing could be more irrational than to give the people power, and to withhold from them information without which power is abused. A people who mean to be their own governors must arm themselves with power which knowledge gives. A popular government without popular knowledge or the means of acquiring it is but a prologue to a farce or a tragedy, or perhaps both.[3]

The First Amendment has always occupied a special position in America. The Supreme Court has repeatedly emphasized the "preferred place given in our scheme to the great, the indispensable freedoms secured by the First Amendment."[4] Without a free press, there can be no freedom, no liberty, no democracy.

A free press should be given the broadest scope that can be countenanced in an orderly society. The First Amendment is not a guarantee that simply prohibits the government from smashing printing presses. To the contrary:

> The only conclusion supported by history is that the unqualified prohibitions laid down by the framers were intended to give to liberty of the press . . . the broadest scope that could be countenanced in an orderly society. (*Bridges v. California*, 314 U.S. 252, 256, 1941.)

The framers of the Constitution intended that nothing should interfere with the guarantee of freedom of the press. The Amendment is not restricted to protecting the freedoms from "any particular way" of abridging them[5] and has been interpreted as protecting against *indirect* abridgments:

> The fact that no direct restraint or punishment is imposed upon speech or assembly does not determine the free speech question. Under some circumstances, indirect "discouragements" undoubtedly have the same coercive effect upon the exercise of First Amendment rights as imprisonment, fines, injunctions, or taxes. (*American Communications Association v. Douds*, 339 U.S. 382, 402, 1950.)

The Court has ruled that even "minor" abridgments are not to be tolerated:

> But inhibition as well as prohibition against the exercise of precious First Amendment rights is a power

denied to government. . . . we cannot sustain an intrusion
on First Amendment rights on the ground that the intrusion is only a minor one. (*Boyd v. U.S.,* 116 U.S.
616, 635, 1886).

"Unintended" restraints on a free press are not excused
either:

> Abridgment of such rights (of free speech, press, and
> association) even though unintended, may inevitably
> follow from varied forms of governmental action. 102
> (*NAACP v. Alabama ex rel Patterson,* 357 U.S. 449,
> 461, 1958.)

In recent years the concept of freedom of the press has
included the public's right *to receive* information:

> It is the right of the viewers and listeners, not the
> right of the broadcasters, which is paramount . . . It is
> the right of the public to receive suitable access to social,
> political, esthetic, moral, and other ideas and experiences
> which is crucial here. (*Red Lion Broadcasting Co. v.
> FCC,* 395 U.S. 367, 390, 1969.)

A right to receive information is firmly based in the First
Amendment, according to Justice William J. Brennan, Jr.:

> It is true that the First Amendment contains no spe-
> cific guarantee of access to publications. However, the
> protection of the Bill of Rights goes beyond the specific
> guarantees to protect from Congressional abridgment
> those equally fundamental personal rights necessary to
> make the express guarantees fully meaningful. I think
> the right to receive publications is such a fundamental
> right. The dissemination of ideas can accomplish noth-
> ing if otherwise willing addressees are not free to re-
> ceive and consider them. It would be a barren market-

place of ideas that had only sellers and no buyers.
(*Lamont v. Postmaster General*, 381 U.S. 301, 308,
1965.)

If the First Amendment is to be effective, it must ensure
that Americans receive "the widest possible dissemination
of information from diverse and antagonistic sources."[6] As
the government becomes a more pervasive influence in our
society, and as that society itself becomes more complex,
the need for a free flow of information increases. Channels
of communication in America must remain free and open
if we are to continue to seek the ideal envisioned in the
Constitution.

*Information received from confidential sources is an
integral part of modern news-gathering operations.* This
premise and the one to follow are probably the two most
important in the rationale for a privilege law. The premise
itself is simple: in order to provide citizens with "the widest
possible dissemination of information," confidential sources
are essential.

Most citizens realize reporters receive confidential "tips"
or other information from sources who do not wish to be
identified publicly. Journalist Curtis MacDougall has
briefly outlined the process a reporter may use to get a
story:

> A newspaper on the trail of an important item must
> be very judicious in deciding which of its news sources it
> is going to approach. Not infrequently a reporter has
> something like this to say to one of his best informants:
> "The office has gotten wind of such and such a story,
> and is going to use a writeup. I know you won't like it
> but I can't do anything about it, so how about helping
> me since it's going to appear anyway?"
> Such tactics may work once in a while, but they can-
> not be overworked without arousing suspicion or without

closing too many important mouths. The value of the
ordinary beat reporter, the one who covers an important
source such as police headquarters or city hall, depends
in large part upon his ability to make and keep friends
who are willing to take him into their confidence.[7]

Of course, the reporter doesn't always solicit the confidential information. Sometimes the sources come to a well-
known newsman in a particular locale, and after receiving
assurances that he can be trusted, reveal information of
some news value.

In either instance, the reporter must maintain his confidences for reasons other than honor: if he does not abide
by the journalist's code of ethics, he will rapidly lose many
valuable contacts. As MacDougall explains:

> Once their promise is given they would rather go to
> jail, as many of them have, than break it [the code of
> ethics]. The reporter who didn't live up to this code
> would find himself without "pipelines," and his effective-
> ness would be reduced greatly. Experience proves that
> the person with whom the reporter "plays ball" on one
> occasion is likely to supply the tip which leads to a better
> story on another.[8]

Today, both broadcast and print journalists depend upon
confidential information *daily* in gathering, researching
and producing the news.

CBS News anchorman Walter Cronkite has stressed the
importance of confidential information:

> In doing my work, I (and those who assist me) de-
> pend constantly on information, ideas, leads, and opin-
> ions received in confidence. Such material is essential in
> digging out newsworthy facts and, equally important, in
> assessing the importance and analyzing the significance

of public events. Without such materials, I would be able to do little more than broadcast press releases and public statements.[9]

CBS News reporter Dan Rather also emphasized the necessity of getting confidential information:

> A reporter can know all the facts and still not know the truth. In order to understand the facts, reporters must constantly appraise the accuracy and meaning of words and the significance of deeds. In that effort, reporters require a background of confidential judgments and observations obtainable only in privacy and in trust.[10]

The managing editor of the *New York Times*, A.M. Rosenthal, told me: "Not a day goes by but that the *Times* and other newspapers print stories based on confidential information of one kind or another from confidential sources."[11]

The *Boston Globe*, according to editorial-page editor Charles Whipple, "publishes articles based primarily on information from confidential sources very frequently—sometimes daily and at least once a week."[12]

Reg Murphy, editor of the *Atlanta Constitution*, said, "I doubt that *The Constitution* has published a full edition in the last five years which did not contain confidential information."[13]

"The *Chicago Tribune* probably publishes six to eight stories a month containing information from confidential sources," said editor Clayton Kirkpatrick.[14]

According to executive editor James Bucknam,[15] stories based on confidential information appear "in one or more stories in practically every edition" of the *Manchester Union-Leader*.

But what *kind* of information does the public receive as a result of the journalistic use of confidential sources?

Historically, as the previous chapter illustrated, confidential information has enabled newsmen to provide the public with valuable data on corruption, crime and inefficiency in high places—particularly in government. The cases cited include many instances in which reporters publicly exposed wrongdoing. In addition, journalists have, of course, published many stories based on confidential information without being brought to court to be asked for their sources.

A typical example of the journalistic use of confidential information occurred in the mid–1950s. A group of Houston police officers were stealing narcotics from arrested suspects and selling them for large sums of money. The story was published in the newspapers because honest policemen talked to a trusted reporter.

Walter Cronkite has given two examples of the stories he has uncovered through confidential sources:

> A bartender told me of fraud in restaurant inspection in New York City. A scientist asserted that the Atomic Energy Commission's safety standards for atomic energy installations were not adequate. None of these persons would have volunteered this information if he thought he would be exposed as a source of the information.[16]

Cronkite's colleague Mike Wallace described an instance where confidential information was crucial for a story:

> I recently participated in the preparation of a report for "60 Minutes" relating to the cost overrun on the Mark-48 Torpedo. Some of the most important and revealing information that we obtained came in confidence from subcontractors, suppliers, and men employed by government agencies. Without that information we could not have constructed the story of how a torpedo project originally scheduled to cost $680 million had risen to a projected $4 billion.[17]

Articles in the nation's newspapers in recent years indicate the kinds of stories which have appeared in print as a result of confidential information. In St. Louis, for instance, the *Post-Dispatch* published a series in 1971 about collusive bidding on various highway projects in Illinois. *Post-Dispatch* executive editor Arthur Bertelson told me that the reporter writing the series "had access to a number of informants whose welfare, perhaps even their physical well-being, would be threatened by disclosure of their names."[18] The same reporter covered the Krebiozen "cancer cure" trial several years ago, and "through long and detailed investigation, he was able to publish a series of stories that led to the conviction of the [jury] foreman."[19]

In Philadelphia the *Inquirer* has published a variety of major stories involving confidential information. The "strange workings" of City Bank, Philadelphia's first state-chartered bank in forty years, were revealed in an *Inquirer* series.[20] And confidential information was essential for an *Inquirer* series which revealed the excessive cost of Philadelphia's new Veterans Stadium. The articles pinpointed "the unsafe materials, faulty workmanship and slipshod inspection procedures" used in the new structure as well.[21]

In Chicago the *Tribune* recently published articles on cheating in the cashing of welfare checks. The stories, according to editor Clayton Kirkpatrick, "were based on a confidential report, and there were attempts to force the *Tribune* to disclose its source. These attempts were resisted."[22]

In Atlanta the *Constitution* used confidential information in articles on "the operation of mental health treatment facilities, veterans hospitals, vocational rehabilitation programs, model cities developments, to mention only a few recent series."[23]

In Boston the *Globe* published a series of stories on how, in the city of Somerville, Massachusetts, "millions of dollars went to favored contractors without public, competitive bidding, through the device of splitting contracts so that each was small enough to evade the public bidding law."[24] A team of *Globe* reporters also dug up deals by the Massachusetts Turnpike Authority, and the Authority's exemption from public bidding was ended by the state legislature.[25] The *Globe*'s four-man investigative team during its first year in operation published articles that resulted in 199 indictments against twenty-seven people, including three former city mayors and a city auditor.

In Los Angeles the *Times* has published numerous stories during the past several years on subject matter that would never have reached the public without the use of confidential sources. William Niese, an attorney for the *Times*, said:

> It is difficult to arrange in categories the types of articles based on confidential information. They cover a broad range of subjects, including the operations of all aspects of local, state, and federal government, the activities of private groups, investigations of various kinds, and the list could be extended indefinitely.[26]

Niese did cite several examples of stories that could not have been written "if the confidentiality of sources were not protected" (California has a state privilege law):

> (1) July 26, 1968: an article by John Goldman reported the plans of the demonstrators at the 1968 Democratic National Convention; Goldman informed readers of the activities of leaders of the demonstration, "who met quietly in Cleveland" and decided, according to one unnamed leader, "we're going, the show is on."
>
> (2) May 15, 1969: an article by Ronald Ostrow reported that Supreme Court Justice Abe Fortas agreed to receive $20,000 a year for life from the family foundation of Louis Wolfson.

(3) February 22, 1970: an article by John Goldman and Robert Jackson indicated that U. S. accounts aided the black market in Vietnam and explained how millions of dollars found its way from the U. S. government into the Saigon black market.

(4) February 13, 1970: an article by Jack Nelson reported that the FBI and Meridan police paid $36,500 to two Ku Klux Klan informants to arrange a trap for two Klan terrorists.

(5) February 2, 1971: an article by Stuart Loory examined the status of U. S. intelligence operations in Vietnam following the disastrous raid on Son Tay prison.

Other articles mentioned by Niese included a series about city commissioners, which resulted in indictments, convictions and a Pulitzer Prize; a study of the *Queen Mary* conversion; several stories regarding the operations of the state legislature, which resulted in changes in the legislature's operations; and a study of the extent of Black Panther operations in Southern California.[27]

Richard Oliver of the *New York Daily News*, and cochairman of the Freedom of the Press Committee, explained a recent story the *News* secured from confidential sources:

> Right now my newspaper is engaged in a long-range investigation into the hiring irregularities by the local government in New York City. Without going into too much detail I must tell you the inquiry was begun, in part, as a result of a source—in this instance, a city employee who said he was disgusted with some of the practices he saw going on around him with respect to personnel.
>
> This source came to us with copies of documents and told us his story. But before he did so, he asked that his identity be held in the strictest confidence because he feared for his job. We agreed.

Largely as a result of the information we subsequently received, investigated, and published, several official inquiries were begun and are now continuing into the city's administration of the Federal Emergency Employment Act.

And last week the city announced that it had fired or suspended 11 employees allegedly involved in the falsification of addresses to secure EEA jobs in city government.

This could not have happened unless that initial source came forward and, more importantly, unless he could be assured that his identity would be kept in the strictest confidence.[28]

The press has also relied on confidential information to educate the public about drugs, drug users, radical political groups and other "underground" subjects. The *Philadelphia Inquirer* series of recent articles about Philadelphia's drug problem for example, according to executive editor John McMullan, "would not have been possible without the aid of confidential informants."[29]

Confidential information is also essential in covering foreign affairs. One of the nation's most highly regarded reporters, Max Frankel of the *New York Times*, has said that "there could be no adequate diplomatic, military and political reporting of the kind our people take for granted, without reliance on confidential sources." He observed:

In the field of foreign affairs, only rarely does our Government give full public information to the press for the direct purpose of simply informing the people. For the most part, the press obtains significant information bearing on foreign policy only because it has managed to make itself a party to confidential materials . . .[30]

Since so much information regarding foreign policy and the foreign activities of the United States is secret, citizens must rely on the press to provide them with information. The press, in turn, must constantly utilize confidential sources and information.

Of course, as the *Philadelphia Inquirer*'s McMullan has observed, "Many confidential news tips don't pan out and simply wind up in the waste basket."[31] Responsible reporters always verify information they receive in confidence, to ensure that they are printing facts instead of rumors.

Confidential information frequently does not produce a "big" story but instead a relatively minor one, of importance perhaps to a particular group or community but not of city- or nation-wide significance. Executive editor Arthur Bertelson of the *St. Louis Post-Dispatch* has cited some examples of this:

> Some of the decisions of the St. Louis Symphony Board are regarded by the board as sensitive and therefore not fodder for the newspapers. The same thing applies to the operation of the United Fund in St. Louis, and there are cases where the complaints of tenants in private or semi-public housing are worthwhile to us. If we disclosed the source of some of these stories, our information would dry up and the City of St. Louis and its environs would be the poorer.[32]

Confidential information is also used by reporters to check the validity of their facts and by journalists and news analysts to give a more complete picture in their commentaries or stories. This function is an extremely important one. Yet it is the least known and understood because of its relatively low visibility. A front-page story about graft in City Hall is an obvious example of the benefit the public receives from confidential information; the nuances or tone of an editorial or commentary that are the result of confidential information are difficult, if not impossible, for the public to detect.

Mike Wallace has given an excellent illustration of how this works:

> In the course of my assignment to cover Richard M. Nixon in the early stages of the 1968 campaign, I was present at non-public conversations and conferences and was able to talk informally with the candidate and some of his advisers, including the present Attorney General [John Mitchell]. Although it was seldom explicitly stated, it was understood that some of what was said on those occasions was not for publication. Because of the informality of such discussions, the language used was more casual than that the candidate would use in public. Moreover, ideas were discussed which were tentative and would later be refined or rejected. Had there been any thought at the time that I could be compelled to divulge a full report of some of those meetings, my presence would never have been permitted. As it was, I was able in the course of those sessions to acquire an understanding of the candidate which contributed significantly to my coverage of the campaign and, perhaps more important, an understanding of the President, which has been invaluable in attempting to assess and analyze the present administration.[33]

The information received by a reporter in confidence can often lead to other sources and stories as well. Some of the specific ways in which confidential information is useful in an "indirect" sense were cited by Professor Vince Blasi, a University of Michigan law professor who produced a study report on subpoenas for the Reporters' Committee for Freedom of the Press:

> Information received in confidence is regularly used to verify printable items received from other sources on the record. Off-the-record information is important also

in deciding what emphasis to give certain printable facts in writing up a story; in determining what stories to cover with what commitment of resources; in persuading editors to run a particular story or to give it a certain prominence; and in assessing for the reader the significance of recent developments and the alternatives and probabilities for the future. Confidential information is also helpful to journalists in eliciting on-the-record information from other sources. Confidential tips often lead reporters to those other sources; newsmen sometimes get reluctant sources to talk either by establishing a rapport by means of name-dropping or fact-dropping, or else by convincing the source that the cat is already out of the bag ("I have learned X, can you verify it," or "When will X be announced?").[34]

Thus, information received from confidential sources not only provides the public with important facts; it also enables journalists and commentators to report and interpret with greater clarity and accuracy.

Without a legal privilege for journalists, public access to valuable information is imperiled. There is no single criterion potential sources use in deciding whether or not to provide information to the news media. It is probable, however, that most informants will talk only if the journalist is trusted and/or legally protected from government subpoena. Some sources will talk with a trusted journalist even if there are no assurances of legal protection. On the other hand, if a source's job, security or life are on the line, trust will often not be enough. A journalist might "crack" in front of a tough grand jury. And, even if he were to remain steadfast, the source might feel compelled to unmask himself if he knew his reporter friend would have to go to jail on his account.

An illustration of the "chilling effect" that the use and sanction of subpoenas for reporters creates was provided by *Newsweek* reporter Frank Morgan's account of his interview with one of his sources:

> In connection with the *Newsweek* Magazine February 23, 1970 cover story on the Black Panthers, I made an appointment to interview a physician, who is a Professor of Medicine at a major medical college, and who is nationally acknowledged as a preeminent authority on race relations.
>
> I had interviewed this particular source in connection with stories concerning the "Black Revolution" on at least six separate occasions in the past, and had always found him helpful, cooperative, accurate and an excellent source for stories of mine dealing with Blacks. Quite apart from my reportorial duties, I had become acquainted with my source socially and had met him informally on a number of occasions.
>
> On the date of my appointment, February 6, 1970, I arrived at my source's office and, in preparation for the interview, began, as usual, to set up my tape recorder. My source told me that he did not want our conversation taped. I explained that recordation of the interview was for my source's protection as well as mine, and that, in discussing with him such technical matters as the psychological bases for Black Pantherism, I was anxious to achieve absolute accuracy.
>
> My source persisted in refusing to allow me to tape our interview. He asked me what protection he would have if I even took notes, and expressed concern that my notes and the full story I filed might be subpoenaed by the government—this in spite of the fact that my source conceded that he would not be telling me anything which could be characterized as radical or controversial, or which *Newsweek* Magazine had not previously attributed to him.
>
> I explained to my source that, without notes, I could not prepare and file a story, and there was therefore no point in conducting the interview.

My source finally agreed to be interviewed, but only on condition that I would permit him to review and edit the story I intended to file before I transmitted it to *Newsweek* Magazine's office. Since I felt that, even under these conditions, my source could make a useful contribution to my story, I agreed to these conditions—conditions which I have never before accepted.

As one might expect, my source was extraordinarily guarded in his statements to me and the interview was for my purposes less than satisfactory.

My source told me that his concern stemmed from the "spate of stories" which had appeared that week concerning the issuance of subpoenas requiring production of newsmen's notes and files.

I promised my source that I would honor the traditional confidential relationship and resist fully any attempt by anyone to subpoena any of my materials relating to our interview. My source's fears were not assuaged. He told me that he feared reprisals for what he might say.[35]

A potential informant's concern about concealing his identity is well founded. Syndicated columnist Jack Anderson once published a story that described how Pentagon officials laughed, sang and told dirty jokes as they composed the list of persons to be fired at Christmas time in 1970. The Defense Department denied the story, but Anderson offered to produce a tape of the meeting.

The FBI was called in, and a Pentagon employee named Gene Smith was considered the prime suspect in tape-recording the meeting. As Anderson's associate Brit Hume pointed out:

He [Smith] was grilled mercilessly by military investigators. The FBI visited his neighbors to ask about his drinking habits, his loyalty, his relatives and associates. Before the grand jury, however, Smith denied under oath that he even knew Jack Anderson. U. S. Attorney Brian

Gettings acknowledged afterward to Anderson associate Les Whitten that "we probably do have the wrong man." They did.[36]

Another example indicates what may happen if an informant does not take extraordinary precautions to protect his identity from being revealed. The principal source in a *Los Angeles Times* series allowed the *Times* to quote him and the facts and figures he cited; two convictions of public officials and a major change in the procedures of a million-dollar government agency were the result. The source who performed this public service was immediately fired by the agency's directors after twenty-seven years of service. It was only after two years of litigation and public pressure that he was able to get his job back.[37]

The *Los Angeles Times* also persuaded a businessman to reveal how he did business with a public agency. The source remained confidential, "for he wanted to continue to be a businessman."[38] Recently he called the editor of the *Times*, William Thomas, although the article he had provided information for had been published long before. He wanted to know if the stories about judges and newsmen's sources would result in the retroactive revelation of his identity: "He was serious, and he was afraid."[39]

Editors and reporters throughout the country realize that their position is a precarious one. At the annual meeting of editors and bureau chiefs of the *Wall Street Journal* in October 1972, managing editor G. Frederick Taylor "told people that they want to understand that when they promise somebody that they won't use their name, more than at any other time in the history of the republic, this opens up the possibility of going to jail, and they should not do it casually."[40]

In fact, the fear that potential sources now feel is shared by some reporters.

A well-known Washington free-lance author abandoned the idea of doing an article about a friend deeply involved in the soft-drug traffic:

> Because the man had strong philosophical, rather than financial, reasons for his activity, the writer thought his case would be interesting. His friend was eager for the public to hear his views and agreed to cooperate if he were not identified. When the Court ruling [*Branzburg v. Hayes*] came down, however, the writer changed his mind. "I never even considered doing it after that," he said. In fact, the writer was so intimidated by the prospect of being hauled before a grand jury to identify his friend that he insisted his name not be used in this article.[41]

Before the *Washington Post* published its stories on the Watergate scandal, a writer who has produced front-page stories for the *New York Post* and the *New York Times* stated that he knew the story behind the bugging of Democratic headquarters at the Watergate, but he couldn't report it because "My source says he will deny it, and I've read the Caldwell decision and I don't want to go to jail." [42]

As Victor Navasky of the American Civil Liberties Union observed about this case:

> Since the writer in question first revealed Dan Ellsberg's involvement in the Pentagon Papers, his sources can't be taken lightly and at a minimum we must assume that the public is one hypothesis poorer about who did what at the Watergate, an event which has been treated as a comic opera, but which involves fundamental constitutional and moral issues relating to the right to privacy and the dangers of government surveillance.[43]

Many reporters who cover controversial stories take pains to destroy any notes or materials that might be sub-

ject to subpoena. For example, one of the authors of a
Look magazine article that linked San Francisco Mayor
Joseph Alioto with the Mafia refused to reveal confidential
information—but he also ensured that the authorities
could not force him to divulge it. He cut the names of his
informants out of his notebooks and "burned some and
washed the others down a sewer."[44]

The *St. Louis Post-Dispatch* institutionalized Brisson's
policy with regard to photographs after a government subpoena for *Post-Dispatch* photographs of a demonstration:

> . . . we have made it company policy to destroy all prints
> and negatives within three days so that we will not be in
> a position of having to provide information that a pro-
> secutor can use to make a case against someone who may
> not have been in the least involved. This provides a de-
> gree of hardship for us since there are many occasions
> when it would be helpful to have the prints or negatives
> that we now must destroy.[45]

It was the Supreme Court that emphasized in 1963 (in
the case of *NAACP v. Button*) that First Amendment
freedoms "are delicate and vulnerable, as well as supremely
precious in our society. The threat of sanctions may deter
their exercise almost as potently as the actual application
of sanctions."[46]

It is impossible to determine how often information does
not reach a reporter because a potential source feels threatened, but there are undoubtedly many important stories
that the public will never know of because the risk of identification is becoming too great in the minds of many
sources.

In 1970, for example, ABC News reporter Timothy
Knight was forced to cancel a proposed documentary on
the Black Panthers. The Panthers insisted that ABC pledge

to fight any subpoena issued by the government because of the documentary, but the network refused to make the pledge, and the Panthers were afraid to cooperate.[47]

Newsweek reporter Min Yee was faced with a similar situation when he accompanied a group of young American radicals who were going to Cuba as volunteers to cut sugar cane. Yee was forced to flee Cuba, leaving his notes and film behind, because the young people thought that the American government would successfully force him to reveal the information he had gathered. According to Yee, they said to him, "What if Pig Mitchell [the Attorney General at that time] sticks a gun in your stomach and says, 'Give me your film.' You're going to hand it over, right?"[48]

Reporter Larry Dickinson of the *Baton Rouge State Times* claims that a story on corruption in Louisiana politics was lost because the potential source feared the subpoena threat. "Arguments that used to be easy—that you would protect them and so forth—now become more difficult," he said.[49]

In his testimony before a House of Representatives subcommittee, William Small, vice-president of CBS News and Chief of the CBS Washington Bureau, cited an example of the constriction of the flow of information without a legal privilege:

> This is a memo from Isaac Kleinerman, who is one of our most distinguished documentarians. He was working on a story down in Georgia, part of it having to do with children, and he wrote a memo saying that he wanted to see what happened to children of welfare families, and talks about a Georgia law which says that the family cannot receive welfare if the husband is residing with the family, so there is much fraudulent collection of welfare with the husband allegedly not but actually still residing there.
>
> He said he found such a family and a situation in

which the woman was willing to tell her story on camera, providing we could guarantee her anonymity, and he was able to tell her she would be photographed in such a way and place that no one could recognize her and indeed he could even alter the quality of her voice on the sound track so it would not be recognizable. And then he said this was not able to placate her since she was aware of the Supreme Court ruling in the Caldwell case. Her point was that, after the program was aired, the Georgia authorities would come to CBS and demand that we reveal her identity. This would then make her subject to prosecution for fraud and force her to make restitution for all the money she had received from the welfare department.

[Mr. Conyers, subcommittee member, then asked:] If CBS revealed their sources?

Correct. He then called people in New York and asked for the CBS position, and was told that indeed there could be no guarantee that if he, this producer, Mr. Kleinerman, were subpoenaed, he would either divulge the woman's name or be subject to being placed in jail, a thought which did not appeal, he said.

So he has abandoned the interview and concludes: "We were not able to film the woman, and consequently lost what might have been a valuable sequence for our broadcast."[50]

Newsweek reporter John Lowell has declared that he has experienced increasing difficulty in obtaining information from "confidential informants who have cooperated with me fully and with no reluctance in the past." Lowell also observed that sometimes "these sources tacitly acknowledge they possess newsworthy information by responding to my questions with such statements as 'I wish I could tell you that.'"[51]

In the course of producing his report Vince Blasi talked with scores of reporters who gave him examples of stories lost because of the subpoena threat:

"[t]he incident (being subpoenaed) and subsequent publicity cost me several good sources on the fringe of the underworld. The loss was measurable."

"In a recent investigation of court corruption in Chicago, several persons with first-hand knowledge of fixes in civil personal injury cases refused to talk in specifics despite assurances that I would not testify as to my sources."

"Three instances come into mind quickly—a story that I did on draft dodgers in Canada, a story on Black Panther demonstrations at Yale, and a story involving an anti-war demonstration in Washington."

"Once, in covering a bank failure, a teller who was worried that any information he would give me would eventually expose him refused to come through at the last moment, even though he really wanted to make the information public. The information itself could not be traced to him. He was fearful though that I would be forced to identify him in court as my news source."

"Story involving draft resisters in federal prison, who refused to relate certain allegedly illegal practices."[52]

Without a journalists' privilege, potential sources become hesitant, reluctant, and often just plain scared. Reporters, too, feel the effects of the threat of a choice between breaking a confidence or serving a jail term. The result? Sources don't talk. Reporters don't pursue stories which may cause them trouble. The public doesn't get the information it is entitled to have.

8

The Case for a Journalistic Shield

FEDERAL SUBPOENAS of reporters' notes and communications with sources threaten both the free flow of news to the public and independence of the press. When a subpoena is issued by the government to a journalist or news organization, the journalist or organization immediately becomes a willing or unwilling agent of the government. If the press does not remain independent of government influence, control and domination, it cannot serve its vital function in a free society. As the *New York Times* observed editorially:

> If the press is to fulfill the independent role guaranteed to it by the First Amendment, the line of separation between it and the Government must be kept unmistake-

able. That line is jeopardized by the subpoenas various news magazines, television networks, and newspapers, including *The New York Times*, have recently received from Federal authorities for notes, files, film, and other material.[1]

The stifling effect of a government subpoena is felt regardless of the confidentiality of the information requested. For example, the government might seek to subpoena a news photographer's film of a demonstration against the President's trip to Communist China. A variety of repercussions would result from this seemingly innocuous demand for nonconfidential news film.

First, the subpoena will cost the photographer and the news organization that employs him valuable time and money, particularly if they decide to fight the issue in court. Both the time and the money are diverted from the journalist's and organization's normal task: providing the public with news.

In many instances, the cost of fighting a subpoena may be the most significant factor in a journalist's or publication's decision about whether or not to enter a legal battle. The *Los Angeles Times*, for example, has spent "well in excess of $100,000" between 1969 and 1973 fighting subpoenas.[2] Since the *Times* is one of the nation's largest newspapers, it can afford to allocate such sums to legal expenses, though it probably hurts. For thousands of small local newspapers, however, *any* legal fees would be staggering. It is understandable that such news organizations seek to avoid legal difficulties at virtually any cost. A subpoena fight could well be fatal—even if the newspaper *won*.

Second, potential demonstrators will also have "second thoughts" before they express their grievances against the government publicly because they know that anyone with a camera—even if he is from a major television network—

is recording the event for the government. Not only the participants in the subpoenaed film, but all citizens—any citizen who has ever contemplated public protest—will be imbued with the extremely subtle yet alarmingly potent suggestion that "the government is watching," and "you'd better think twice."

Third, the photographer and organization involved will have "second thoughts" about filming such occurrences again, and other journalists will be similarly affected to some degree. Even if a journalist does not respond consciously to the subpoena, he will undoubtedly retain a degree of subconscious reluctance to place himself in the position of the subpoenaed photographer; he is not absolutely deterred from gathering the news but he might have "second thoughts" about filming or reporting certain events.

An example of the effect of a government subpoena on one news organization was cited by John Wicklein, a former New York newsman for WCBS-TV:

> There was a tremendous fear of what the administration could do to that broadcasting station in terms of harassing it. The executives quite clearly stated that they felt CBS was the number one target of the administration. They really got their lawyers into everything. They said, in effect, to newsmen: "Don't do anything that could get us a complaint." People in the newsroom were just scared silly of controversy. They thought the network would like very much to get out of the area of controversy and into nothing but entertainment. In fact, there are some people there who think the network would like to get out of news altogether. I think the hard news has been destroyed there.[3]

When reporters or news organizations are no longer willing or able to pursue stories that may be controversial, or that may damage the image of a mayor, a governor or a President, the theoretical chilling effect has become very real.

The independence of the media can be assured only if reporters are not placed in the compromising position of performing two functions—one of informing the public of the news and the other of providing evidence for government investigators and prosecutors. An analogy can be made to wiretapping. Wiretapped conversations are not permitted as evidence in court under normal circumstances because people cannot be free if they must worry about whether their private telephone conversations are being monitored by a government agent. If reporters are subpoenaed by the government to provide information, they become walking wiretap devices. No one can talk to a reporter, even in confidence, and be certain that the conversation is not being "tapped."

To some, the fact that journalists assist law-enforcement agencies or prosecutors in their activities may not seem so bad; after all, it can be argued, the reporters are only doing a civic duty by becoming ad hoc investigators for the police.

Possibly, in some respects, "law enforcement" would be "improved" by such a development. But the American experiment in democracy would be undermined. There are many actions that could be taken to improve law enforcement: police could randomly frisk citizens on the street, mail could be opened by government investigators, houses could be searched at will by policemen without a warrant. All of these actions are, however, unacceptable in our society.

If valuable freedoms are sacrificed, an improvement in law enforcement is of no value. With the press no longer independent of the government, one of our most valuable freedoms would be destroyed. As the *Columbia Journalism*

Review observed: "The question is . . . whether American journalism can hope to fulfill its First Amendment mission if newsmen are suspected of being akin to the Soviet journalist-spies-informers described by former Moscow correspondent Aaron Einfrank in *Notes on the Art*."[4]

Ironically, if reporters become perceived as extensions of the government, the net effect will be to hinder rather than help law enforcement. Sources will "dry up," and reporters will have nothing to provide to the police. More important, however, is that their service as investigative journalists would be destroyed—and that service contributes mightily to the cause of law enforcement. As previously noted, the *Boston Globe* investigative reporting team published stories in one year that resulted in 119 indictments against twenty-seven people—and they did so by using confidential sources and information. Investigative reporters for other newspapers have produced similar results. The press can best serve society and law-enforcement agencies by doing the job it is intended to do: to independently report and uncover the news. If the press is free to do that, it will unquestionably enlighten the public and the police about the problems of crime in the society. If it must relinquish its independence to provide information directly to the police, no one will benefit.

Government subpoenas threaten the information media at a time when their independence is being questioned for other reasons. Many commentators fear that the press has already lost much of its autonomy—that government has become so pervasive and powerful that it has smothered journalists' critical perception. James McCartney, a national correspondent for the Knight newspapers, has argued that the press is constantly "used" by the government to print what the government deems desirable. According to McCartney, a prime example of the press's lack of independence was its coverage of the war in Vietnam:

In retrospect, examples of Pentagon misrepresentation now seem almost inconceivable. Take Defense Secretary Robert McNamara's misrepresentations on the troop buildup. On October 14, 1966, McNamara returned from his eighth "fact finding" mission to South Vietnam and declared, "I see no reason to expect any significant increase in the level or tempo of operations in South Vietnam, nor do I see any reason to believe that deployments of U. S. forces to that country will change significantly in the future."

The number of U. S. troops at that time was 331,000. In the months to come the troop level steadily rose at a rate of more than 10,000 a month—a massive effort. By the following April—six months after McNamara's flat statement—more than 100,000 new troops had been sent to Vietnam. McNamara's remarks were made just three weeks before the 1966 Congressional elections.

The *Times* and other papers, in the traditional manner of the press, reported the statements and figures. They held a mirror up to Lyndon Johnson's declarations and sought to report accurately all that was said.

Wicker [Tom Wicker, the *New York Times* Washington Bureau chief during the period of the escalation], among others, today asks more. It could be that the families of more than 40,000 Americans killed in Vietnam would ask more, too. For it is apparent that the press was often used by the Johnson administration to merchandise its Vietnam policies—policies a majority of the public now believe were a mistake.[5]

McCartney's example does not indicate overt collusion between reporters and government officials to mislead the public. Journalists were reporting "facts" when they reported a speech by an administration official containing information about the war. Yet, as McCartney observes, there is a cogent argument that merely reporting "facts" is not enough if Americans are to be fully informed. The press must strive constantly to view each happening, particularly in government, with a critical, questioning eye, or it cannot effectively play its constitutional role in our society.

It is noteworthy that *accurate* stories about the Vietnam situation were based on confidential information. In a *Los Angeles Times* story on January 14, 1973, Pulitzer Prize Advisory Board secretary John Hohenberg was quoted as saying: "Every Pulitzer Prize won for coverage of the Vietnam War, beginning with those won by Malcolm Brown of the AP and David Halberstam of *The New York Times* in 1964, depended on confidential sources." The same article noted that Seymour Hersh, who won a Pulitzer Prize for breaking the My Lai massacre story for the Dispatch News Service in 1969, relied on confidential sources, including three army officers, a Congressman, and two Congressional aides.

Unfortunately, the task of covering the government is a monstrous one, and it is continuing to grow. One observer has estimated that there are currently twenty million classified government documents, and that 99.5 percent of them could be publicized without affecting national defense.[6] Americans have a right to know, and it will be fulfilled only by aggressive journalism.

The broadcast media in particular are faced with the problem. Licensed by the government, they are acutely sensitive to government subpoenas for *any* information, which can result in a dangerous self-censorship.

The continued absence of legal protection will undermine any efforts by the press to become truly independent. As the law stands today, any government subpoena for a reporter's information—whether confidential or not—will contribute to the chilling effect on the media. And it is of substantial significance that many citizens do not view such a situation with appropriate alarm.

As James Doyle wrote in the *Providence Journal*:

Big and savage attacks on freedom of the press arouse big and savage defenses of the freedom of the press. I am deeply afraid that the most serious threat to an honest, free press will come from the slow erosion of freedom in the name of forced or unforced "cooperation" with the federal police—and then, in sure and slow stages, with state and local police.

The moment a free press allows itself to become an arm of any agency of the government, it will have lost its right to claim freedom and it will shame decency if it cries freedom.[7]

The adoption of a privilege law would help ensure that such a "slow erosion of freedom" does not occur by strengthening the press's ability to maintain its proper independence.

It should also be noted that a federal reporters' privilege law would preclude the possibility of government use of its subpoena power to harass the press or dissident groups. The effects of the legal summons have already been described—in every sense, a subpoena is a tremendous burden on a journalist or organization. It can also be used by officials as a powerful weapon to induce conformity among journalists who are perceived as too critical. The government can issue subpoenas selectively to those members of the information media whom it distrusts or with whom it disagrees. Furthermore, officials can use the tactic to reduce the extent of news coverage given to a particular group. For example, if the John Birch Society began to receive increased publicity by criticizing the government, an official who opposed the Society could subpoena reporters writing articles on the group—and there would almost certainly be a decreasing number of stories about the Birchers and their criticisms.

The idea of such use of government subpoenas is not fanciful. As the history of reporters' privilege cases shows, subpoenas have most frequently been issued by officials who wished to retaliate for unfavorable stories. The American Civil Liberties Union study on press freedom also acknowledged the harassment potential of the subpoena power:

> It is unlikely that a subpoena from the government to a newsman will bring in much more information on a suspected individual or group than the government already has been able to compile, what with its widespread use of under-cover agents, informants, and surveillance devices. More likely, the subpoena is an instrument used to fish for random incriminating information; to harass the reporter who learns too much; to cut down on the amount of "publicity" a dissident group gets; and, to serve notice on the press that the government does not consider it its equal, but rather its enemy.[8]

According to the subpoena study conducted by Vince Blasi:

> Some newsmen believe that when the government subpoenas a reporter, often the primary "interest" it is seeking to advance is its interest in reducing the news coverage given to certain dissident elements in the society. A respondent to our qualitative survey reported, for example, that "[o]ne television executive was told by a U. S. Attorney that if you didn't film this sort of stuff you wouldn't be having this problem."[9]

The institution of the grand jury, regardless of its other functions, is an exceptionally effective device for government harassment. Grand jury proceedings are secret, and their investigations are broad. The grand jury is permitted to probe into any area of suspected criminal activity. As the Supreme Court pointed out, "It is a grand inquest, a body with powers of investigation and inquisition, the scope of whose inquiries is not to be limited narrowly by questions of propriety or forecasts of the probable result of the investigation. . . . [A grand jury] investigation may be triggered by tips, rumors, evidence professed by the prosecutor, or the personal knowledge of the grand jurors."[10]

And according to Justice Stewart, the grand jury is "in effect, immune from judicial supervision." It can be convened by a prosecutor "on virtually any pretext" and "with no serious law enforcement purpose."[11]

Thus, as law professor Lawrence Velvel observed, prosecutors can use grand jury proceedings "to discover the identities of persons who have told reporters about shady deals or rotten policies of the prosecutors's political or governmental allies, or have told reporters about the criminal activities of people who pay off the politicians. Once their names are discovered, the informants can be harassed or lose their jobs or end up in a concrete barrel at the bottom of a river."[12]

As long as grand juries continue to function in the manner described, and as long as journalists can be compelled to reveal information or be sentenced for contempt, the potential for harassment will remain great. Such harassment is an incalculably destructive force. As Justice Douglas wrote in his dissent in the Branzburg case:

> Today's decision is more than a clog upon news gathering. It is a signal to publishers and editors that they should exercise caution in how they use whatever information they can obtain. Without immunity they may be summoned to account for their criticism. Entrenched officers have been quick to crash their powers down upon unfriendly commentators . . .[13]

A testimonial privilege would reduce the possibilities for the harassment of the press by government officials just as it would ensure a free flow of information and an independent press. These are the major reasons for the adoption of legislation to create such privilege for reporters. There are also a number of secondary arguments for the legislation which should be at least briefly acknowledged.

The legislation would give legal recognition to the journalists' code of ethics, and a reporter would no longer be forced to make the painful choice between violating his ethics and breaking the law. As history demonstrates, journalists have almost always chosen to break the law rather than violate the ethics of their profession. So, in the end, the government is not provided with any additional information, and the reporter must pay a fine or serve a term in jail, or both.

A reporter's right to freedom of association would be strengthened by the legislation. If not legally protected from being forced to reveal confidential information, a journalist may lose his right to associate freely with others as a consequence of a subpoena. If a reporter fears a subpoena, he will hesitate to call upon other persons who may be placed in jeopardy if their conversation is revealed publicly. And if a newsman's ability to circulate is destroyed, he is of little value to his employer or the public.

A privilege law would protect the anonymity of a reporter's source. Although the "right to anonymity" is only an emerging concept in the law, recent Supreme Court decisions indicate that there is such a thing as the right to remain anonymous in order to ensure free expression.

In *Talley v. California*,[14] the Court considered the validity of a Los Angeles ordinance that outlawed the distribution of anonymous handbills. The Court reversed the conviction on the ground that the statute's requirement was an unconstitutional restriction of the freedom to distribute the handbills. The Court emphasized the importance of anonymity for press freedom:

Anonymous pamphlets, leaflets, brochures and even books have played an important role in the progress of mankind. Persecuted groups and sects from time to time throughout history have been able to criticize oppressive practices and laws either anonymously or not at all. The obnoxious press licensing law of England, which was also enforced on the Colonies, was due in part to the knowledge that exposure of the names of printers, writers and distributors would lessen the circulation of literature critical of the government. The old seditious libel cases in England show the lengths to which government had to go to find out who was responsible for books that were obnoxious to the rulers. John Lilburne was whipped, pilloried and fined for refusing to answer questions designed to get evidence to convict him or someone else for the secret distribution of books in England. Two Puritan Ministers, John Penry and John Udal, were sentenced to death on charges that they were responsible for writing, printing or publishing books. Before the Revolutionary War colonial patriots frequently had to conceal their authorship or distribution of literature that easily could have brought down on them prosecutions by English-controlled courts. Along about that time the Letters of Junius were written and the identity of their author is unknown to this day. Even the Federalist Papers, written in favor of the adoption of our Constitution, were published under fictitious names.[15]

In *Gibson v. Florida Legislative Investigation Committee*,[16] the Court again reversed a conviction on the ground that anonymity is sometimes necessary to guarantee freedom of expression. A contempt conviction against the NAACP for refusing to disclose membership lists to a committee investigating subversive activities was overturned by the Court.

In sum, the enactment of privilege legislation would ensure that the press is free of government control (however subtle), harassment or even the suggestion of government influence. Only in this way can it serve its constituents: the American people.

9

The Opposition
to a
Journalistic Shield

WHAT ARE THE ARGUMENTS cited *against* enacting a law to shield journalists' sources from government subpoenas?

One of the major tenets of our judicial system is that individuals must testify before a court of law if called upon to do so. The theory is that if all witnesses are required to testify, then it is assured that all relevant information will be introduced into the judicial process and, therefore, the outcome will be the fairest one possible. The duty to testify was recognized in English common law and has been accepted throughout the history of American jurisprudence. However, the requirement is not absolute. Although American courts have been extremely reluctant to establish exceptions, they nevertheless *have* been created.

The recognized legal authority on evidence is the late Northwestern University professor John Henry Wigmore. Wigmore's approach was to assume that there could be no exceptions to the duty to testify and then to proceed to permit exceptions only if they fully justified themselves.[1] Wigmore established four conditions, which he argued must be satisfied in order to justify the creation of any privilege against compulsory testimony:

(1) The communications must originate in a confidence that they will not be disclosed;

(2) This element of confidentiality must be essential to the full and satisfactory maintenance of the relation between the parties;

(3) The relation must be one which in the opinion of the community ought to be sedulously fostered;

(4) The injury that would inure to the relation by the disclosure of the communications must be greater than the benefit thereby gained for the correct disposal of litigation.[2]

Many courts and legal authorities (including Wigmore himself) have rejected a reporters' privilege on the basis that it did not satisfy Wigmore's four conditions. Their argument is as follows:

First, the communications do not originate in a confidence because the whole point of the reporter–source relationship is to reveal information through publication in a newspaper.

Second, confidentiality is not essential to the relationship between a reporter and a source because the relationship can be maintained on a nonconfidential basis.

Third, there is no community interest in fostering the reporter–informant relationship for its own sake.

Fourth, there is no injury suffered when the communication is disclosed because it is intended to be disclosed.

As Massachusetts lawyers James Guest and Alan Stanzler have observed, however, "such a literal application of Wigmore's conditions to the issue of the newsmen's privilege borders on sophistry and dramatically misconstrues the problem."[3] In fact, the argument that the newsmen's privilege *does* satisfy the four conditions is extremely sound.

First, the communications between a reporter and his confidential source must originate in a confidence that they will not be disclosed. Certainly, *all* communications between a journalist and his informants are not confidential (including whatever information is used in the story). Nor, of course, are *all* communications between lawyers, priests, doctors and their sources confidential. Often, however, communications between the reporter and his source are confidential. Most frequently, the source's identity is the confidential information. Thus, while a portion of the information communicated by such a source is for publication, certain information is *not* for publication—and the communications originate in a confidence that this information will not be revealed.

Second, the element of confidentiality is essential to the full and satisfactory maintenance of the relation between the reporter and his source. It is probably *more* essential than it is in any of the legally recognized privileges. Consider the comparison made by Dean Abraham Goldstein of the Yale Law School:

> Most disclosures are made to an attorney because the client wants the best possible advice and because he realizes that he will be the loser if he withholds the raw materials on which such advice should be predicated. The patient tells all to his physician because he wants to be diagnosed and treated properly. Information is given to social workers, teachers, and guidance counselors be-

cause theirs is a problem which calls for help. The persons who make such communications probably know very little about the degree to which their confidences may be disclosed in the future; but if they did, the immediate interest in getting good advice would probably prevail, the communication would be made, and the professional relationships would remain viable.

In the case of the journalist's privilege, the informant does not risk his health or liberty or fortune or soul by withholding information. He is likely to be moved by baser motives—spite or financial reward—or, on occasion, by a laudable desire to serve the public welfare if it can be done without too much jeopardy. His communication, more than the others, is probably the result of a calculation and more likely to be affected by the risk of exposure. In this instance, compelling the disclosure of a confidential source in one highly publicized case really is likely to restrict the flow of information to the news media. And by doing so, it may well interfere with the freedom of the press guaranteed by the First Amendment.[4]

An examination of the kinds of stories resulting from confidential information is evidence of the fact that the element of confidentiality is crucial. If a source reveals information about government corruption and he is an official in the government, the need for confidentiality is clear. It is vital in stories concerning the activities of minority and dissident groups in society. Marijuana users would never have permitted Annette Buchanan to interview them in 1966 if their relationship with her had not been confidential. Earl Caldwell could never have established a relationship with the Black Panthers if it had not been done in confidence.

If a reporter violates a trust—or is even *perceived* as violating a trust—the journalist/source relationship is destroyed. In fact, confidentiality is so important that the consequences of a violation usually extend beyond the immediate relationship.

In 1968 Anthony Ripley covered the national convention of the Students for a Democratic Society for the *New York Times*. About a year later, Ripley was subpoenaed to appear before the House Internal Security Committee (HISC). He told the committee that he was reluctant to testify, but he did so. Two weeks later Ripley covered a street demonstration in Ann Arbor, Michigan. He was interviewing a student when another student came up and said, "Don't talk to him [Ripley]—he's the guy who testified before HUAC (House Un-American Activities Committee, previous name of HISC)." The student then refused to talk further with Ripley.[5]

The 1969 SDS convention was held several weeks after Ripley testified. As a direct result of his testimony, a resolution was presented to the delegates to exclude representatives of the *Times* from all meetings and to require other reporters to sign statements agreeing not to testify before government investigating committees. The resolution criticized Ripley for testifying and said that Ripley and the *Times* "had taken the side of the nation's most notorious witch hunters."[6] The resolution was considered, but a stronger resolution was adopted in its place, barring *all* "establishment" reporters from the convention.

Times reporter John Kifner was forced to cover the five-day convention without actually attending any meetings. His reaction to the experience is instructive:

> Based upon my experience as a news reporter, it is clear to me that when reporters covering dissenting forces in society are forced to testify about them, their neutrality is compromised and all confidence in them is lost. Before a person will talk openly to a reporter, he must

believe that the reporter will respect what is told in confidence. The threat that the reporter may have to disclose such confidences has a chilling effect on his relationship with news sources and, in my opinion, could eventually destroy any possibility of a free flow of information.[7]

Third, the relationship between the journalist and his source is one that "in the opinion of the community ought to be sedulously fostered." A key word in this condition is the term "community." If "community" were defined as comprising only journalists, it could safely be asserted that the "community" believes the reporter/source relationship should be "sedulously fostered." If "community" means only a community of lawyers, the opinion could well be the opposite. The best definition seems obvious: "community" should be synonymous with "society"—the people of the United States. Utilizing such a definition, it is clear that the reporter/source relationship is one the community believes should be fostered.

The people are dependent upon the news media for their information. Without access to the press, people would be unaware of events occurring throughout the world, in the nation and even locally, and citizens would be unable to make reasoned judgments in choosing their elected representatives at all levels of government.

An unquestioned public priority is the receipt of accurate and complete information about the society in which we live. The role of confidential information in providing citizens with this has been demonstrated. NBC president Julian Goodman predicted the results that would occur in a society that did *not* foster a reporter/source relationship:

> We would hear less and less of dissenters and fewer and fewer militant voices—on the streets and in the public forums. Institutions and men—public and private— might appear more nearly perfect because there would

be less focus on their deficiencies and errors. Policies would seem wiser because they would be less subject to public scrutiny. The power of government over the information available to the public would become paramount.[8]

Certainly it is in the interests of the community to foster a relationship that benefits all citizens and contributes to effective and efficient representative government. (That the community supports the relationship between journalists and their sources is not idle theory. Actual cases involving the privilege have demonstrated that public sentiment endorses the efforts of reporters to maintain confidential relationships in gathering the news.[9] The cases during the past several years apparently have awakened some community support: a recent Gallup poll indicated that 57 percent supported a reporters' privilege.[10])

Fourth, "the injury that would inure to the relation by disclosure of the communications must be greater than the benefit thereby gained for the correct disposal of litigation." The issue here extends beyond the injury suffered by the reporter and his source. (Both do sustain injuries, of course. The reporter loses respect among his colleagues, and his ability to gather news is diminished. The source may suffer far graver injuries: the loss of his job, threats of or actual physical injuries.) Beyond this, all of us are injured when confidential information between reporter and source is disclosed: our right to know is impaired. And this injury is greater than the benefit to be gained by the court in receiving the confidential information. Such benefit, except in the rare case of a class-action suit, would affect only the two litigating parties. It is extremely unlikely that any case would turn on the question of the confidential information; it is unlikely that the name of a source would be required for "the correct disposal of litigation." In the

one type of case where such information would be crucial
—a libel action—reporters are required to disclose the
relevant information. Thus, the injuries sustained by disclosure are of far greater consequence than the injuries
involved in the disposal of litigation if the source is not
disclosed.

Furthermore, in most instances, there would not be a
case before the court *at all* except for the fact that an enter-
prising reporter used confidential information for a revealing article!

An in-depth examination of Wigmore's "conditions"
reveals, therefore, that the journalists' privilege does satisfy
the criteria for the establishment of a legal privilege. Wigmore's analysis of testimonial privileges contains an inherent assumption that privileges should *not* be created—a
sensible policy *in most circumstances*. In the case of the
reporter/source relationship, however, the burden of proof
should be shifted. Because of the importance of freedom of
the press and a free flow of information to the public, the
presumption should be *in favor of* a reporters' privilege,
with opponents forced to justify the elimination of the privilege because of a common-law tradition of testimonial
compulsion.

In this framework, the reporters' privilege would be
analogous to the Fifth Amendment right not to testify. The
right "to plead the Fifth" was not established after determining whether or not it satisfied Wigmore's four conditions. Rather, the important values underlying the Fifth
Amendment took precedence over the common-law tradition of compulsory testimony.

In addition to Wigmore's analysis, seven major arguments have been advanced against the adoption of a
journalists' privilege:

*1. The privilege would "hinder the search for truth" in
the courtroom.* The principal argument against the estab-

lishment of a reporters' privilege is that, if individuals are not forced to testify, the court will not have access to all of the information regarding a particular case.

There is validity to the view that courts must receive complete information in order to render just verdicts. However, it must also be recognized that in the case of the reporters' privilege there is a conflict between the "correct disposal of litigation" and the freedom of the press.

In such a conflict, First Amendment values should outweigh a common-law tradition. As James Madison observed, "the state of the press under the common law cannot . . . be the standard of its freedom in the United States."[11]

Privilege opponents might argue, however, that the "correct disposal of litigation" involves the constitutional right to a fair trial, and that therefore the conflict cannot be automatically resolved in favor of a privilege.

The two values must be balanced in the specific context of the reporters' privilege situation to determine which value society should hold to be superior in that situation. Is the reporters' privilege enough of a hindrance to the search for truth in the courtroom that it should not be legally recognized? The answer is no.

First, reporters normally do not reveal confidential information even if they are not protected by a privilege law. Although there are occasions when information is revealed, in the majority of instances the search for truth is "hindered" regardless of the existence of a law. A privilege law would not significantly alter the current situation regarding the search for truth in the courtroom.

Second, the assertion of a privilege by a reporter usually involves the reporter's unwillingness to disclose the name of a confidential source. The information he received from the source results in published news stories in most cases. Therefore, in the vast majority of cases, both the public and the courts possess more information *with* a privilege law than without one, since more sources are willing to talk with newsmen if they are confident that their identities are protected.

Third, a journalist's information is rarely crucial to the administration of justice. The history of privilege cases indicates that the withheld information was virtually always peripheral to the issue before the court, and a recent study concluded that "newsmen seldom possess information that might be considered vital" to the fact-finding endeavors of the courts.[12]

Fourth, even if in a rare case a reporter's information is in some way relevant to the case before the court, there are normally other means of securing the information. Historically, courts and investigatory bodies have reached the truth despite the refusal of reporters to provide requested information—beginning in 1857, when a House committee recommended expulsion for three members, although journalist James Simonton never provided the committee with his confidential information. As the *Columbia Journalism Review* observed in the spring of 1970, after the government had issued several subpoenas to reporters covering activities of the Black Panthers:

> The question is . . . whether American law enforcement agencies, which are the appropriate employers of undercover men, have reached such a low state of efficiency that they cannot maintain their own surveillance of potentially dangerous organizations.[13]

Fifth, in an ironic way, the unevaluated raw materials subpoenaed by the government may "hinder the search for truth" more than the absence of such materials. Information received in confidence by reporters is sometimes false, and a reporter may have jotted down leads he has not verified. The introduction of such information into a trial is likely to hinder the search for truth[14] and damage innocent parties.

Sixth, while legal authorities correctly contend that testimonial privileges must be limited, they recognize some such privileges. In so doing, they implicitly concede that other values are more important than the immediate "search for truth" in court. For example, one obvious means of quickly ascertaining the "truth" would be to force lawyers to divulge confidential communications between themselves and their clients. Society has recognized, however, that the search for truth is less important than the search for justice —and that honest and complete communications between lawyer and client are essential if justice is to prevail. Thus, a privilege has been created for lawyers so that they cannot be penalized for refusing to reveal the information they receive from their clients.

Similarly, evidence introduced as a result of wiretapping would surely be an efficient way to search for the truth. But society has not hesitated to render the job of the policeman, the prosecutor and the court more difficult by prohibiting the introduction of wiretap evidence into court. The prohibition on wiretap evidence unquestionably impedes the "search for truth," but there is a more important value: the right of privacy for all Americans.

The reporters' privilege is certainly as beneficial to society as the existing privileges. In fact, there is an extant privilege directly analogous to the reporters' privilege: that accorded to government informers.

It is ironic that Wigmore, while opposing a reporters' privilege, defends the concept of a testimonial privilege for government informers, arguing that "its soundness cannot be questioned."[15] He states that "law enforcement officers often depend on professional informers to furnish them with a flow of information about critical activities" and

that informers would be subject to great risks if their identities were revealed.[16] The Supreme Court has likewise
sanctioned the informers' privilege because "the purpose of
the privilege is the furtherance and protection of the public
interest in effective law enforcement."[17] The identical
analysis could be made for the reporters' privilege.

2. *Since reporters will not divulge confidential information in any case, there is no need for a privilege that will
create yet another exception to the rule that everyone must
testify.* This argument concedes that the search for truth
in the courtroom would not be affected by a privilege law.
It is alleged that there is no real need for a privilege law:
reporters already defy subpoenas, so let them continue to
do so and go to jail—that is an easier course than establishing another complex testimonial privilege.

But if reporters do not divulge their information, then
the establishment of a privilege could do no harm. And it
would be beneficial in the sense that it would eliminate the
threat of jail for some reporters and the actuality for others.

The lawyers and other individuals who advance this
argument believe that reporters should "accept punishment." As journalist John Hohenberg noted:

> Most lawyers, including a committee of the American
> Bar Association, have consistently opposed the extension
> of such confidentiality statutes. They argue that a policy
> of martyrdom by the journalist—of accepting punish-
> ment rather than to reveal sources—is likely to be a
> greater service to society, whatever the journalist himself
> may think of such a proposition.[18]

This is a peculiar perspective for lawyers to advance. In
fact, the argument should be turned around. Since most
reporters will not reveal sources under any circumstances,
a law should be established which would constitute a decla-
ration of public approval. If a law does not correspond to

society's wishes, it is rendered totally ineffective. Arguing that journalists should accept punishment is like arguing that prohibition should never have been repealed and that people who want to buy drinks should do so and accept punishment if they get caught. It should be a legislative priority to minimize the number of laws that are flagrantly disobeyed and that are not crucial to the preservation of freedom or order. A policy of retaining a subpoena power (which is meaningless in terms of what it achieves, i.e., no evidence) that is not observed by journalists can serve only to encourage disrespect for the institution of law in general.

It is unjust for a society to punish a journalist for refusing to violate a confidence that benefits the society. Certainly the argument that government informers should either be revealed or accept jail sentences for refusing to do so would seem ludicrous to any individual in the law-enforcement field. The argument that it is somehow "just" for reporters to go to jail is equally absurd.

There is also the crucial fact that while journalists normally do not reveal their information, there *are* some instances in which they *do* divulge confidences and the fear of prosecution creates a situation in which journalists and sources become reluctant to engage in relationships with one another. A privilege law would eliminate the fear and thereby ensures a free flow of news to the public.

3. A privilege law would encourage numerous false stories and instances of libel. Such fears are understandable but unrealistic. In the nineteen states that have privilege laws there is no indication of a large number of false or libelous articles.

Journalists generally are extremely responsible individuals; their craft demands accuracy and precision, and they are trained to check their facts. As *Philadelphia Inquirer* executive editor John McMullan stated, "Many confidential news tips don't pan out, of course, and simply wind up in the waste basket."[19] Journalists constantly check and double-check stories, particularly if they contain any potentially libelous statements. There is no reason to suppose that the professional standards would suddenly drop if a privilege law is enacted.

Libel is an extremely sensitive area of the law. If a newsman makes a mistake and prints a libelous statement, he will be held responsible for that statement even if a privilege law is enacted. In states with privilege statutes, courts have ruled that reporters may not use the "reliability of their source" as a defense if they invoke the privilege and refuse to reveal the name of their source.

4. Unlike groups which now possess testimonial privileges, journalists are not screened or licensed in any manner. The argument, in the words of a privilege-law opponent, runs as follows:

> Physicians and lawyers are licensed by the state, and their professional activities are carefully scrutinized by various organizations of their own members. Certainly in the case of clergymen and priests such activity is not warranted or necessary. On the other hand, the nebulous activities of some newsmen are only restricted by the limits of their own zeal or that of their employers. The protection of innocent persons from slander and libel by the unscrupulous newsmen seems more compelling in the public interest than the protection of equally unscrupulous informants.[20]

There are four responses to this argument.

First, the only harm suggested by the absence of a licensing procedure for journalists is that reporters will proceed unimpeded in some kind of libelous rampage. Even under a privilege law, there is sufficient protection against libel, as was pointed out in the argument against the last objection. The presence or absence of a licensing procedure is not a relevant factor in the libel issue.

Second, the "screening procedures" currently applied to members of other privileged groups vary considerably. There is virtually no screening at all for ministers and priests in many states, despite the fact that clergymen have a testimonial privilege. Moreover, the journalist tends to be more aware of the consequences of defamatory actions than any other privileged group member. If any profession does not need screening procedures for a privilege, it is journalism.

Third, the other groups are privileged not because they are screened but because society has recognized that confidentiality is essential to their relationships, and because the value derived from such relationships is considered greater than that from the courtroom testimony, which is legally privileged. There is no inherent benefit in licensing per se. And if there is no foreseeable harm that can arise from unlicensed journalists possessing a privilege, the fact that they are not licensed does not constitute an argument against the adoption of a privilege.

Fourth, the reporters' privilege is unlike existing privileges, except for that granted to government informers. In the case of the journalist, the source is confidential, whereas in other privileged relationships both the professional and the source are known. In the reporter/source relationship, at least a portion of the communication is publicly disclosed—usually a large portion; in the other privileged relationships, the communication is normally completely confidential, with no portion of it disclosed to the public. And in most privilege situations, it is the source who invokes the privilege; in the case of the reporters' privilege, it is the journalist who possesses the testimonial privilege.

5. *If a privilege law is enacted, law enforcement efforts will be hampered.* The major premise of this argument is that journalists' confidential sources play a vital role in prosecuting criminals. Without access to reporters' files, the names of criminals will be sheltered and law-enforcement

officers will have their "hands tied." There is no validity to this contention.

There is no indication that crime has increased or gone increasingly undetected in those states that have enacted privilege legislation. Although the chief law-enforcement officers of some states believe the statutes are detrimental,[21] most attorneys general have had no problems with the laws.[22]

Ohio Attorney General William Brown said, "I can think of no instance in which this law (the Ohio shield law) has interfered with my ability to perform the statutory duties of my office."[23]

Alaska Attorney General John Havelock made similar observations about Alaska's shield statute:

> On a working level, all of Alaska's district attorneys say that they have encountered no difficulties because of the newsman's privilege statute; the principal reason, as identified by one district attorney, is that the investigations of law enforcement agencies are so far ahead of the newspapers that prosecuting attorneys have never been compelled to rely on newspaper reporters for information concerning the commission of a crime.[24]

And Michigan Attorney General Frank Kelley stated simply: "This law (the Michigan privilege law) has not interfered in any way with our ability to do our job."[25]

Carol Vance, district attorney of Houston and president of the National District Attorneys Association, said, "There's no doubt that reporters need their confidential sources the same as law enforcement people do. The need is very similar."[26]

In proportion to the totality of the testimonial evidence, testimony from journalists is used infrequently in the courtroom (even though an increasing number of reporters are being subpoenaed), which indicates that such testimony is rarely vital and that its loss would not be significant.

And since reporters actually reveal information very infrequently, a privilege law would not preclude any significant amount of testimony that is being heard without such a law.

If a privilege law has any effect at all on crime, it will be to *diminish* crime, or at least to increase the rate of detection. In the state of Arkansas, one of the primary arguments *in favor* of a privilege statute was that its enactment would tend to *increase* the number of successful prosecutions:

> The Commission [Arkansas Criminal Law Reform Commission] was convinced that undercover criminal activities which might have political or economic protection in a community were more likely to be brought to light, and ultimately prosecuted, if news reporters were given the freedom which the section [privilege statute] authorizes.[27]

6. *The privilege law would favor a business enterprise and would be used to increase the sale of newspapers.* This argument suggests that journalists do not seek legal protection for the benefit of the public but, instead, to sell more newspapers. By publishing exposés and other stories based on confidential information protected by the law, newspapers, it is contended, will attract new readers, new advertisers and, ultimately, new dollars. There are two basic responses to this objection.

First, it is not the "business enterprise" that is protected by a privilege law, but only the confidential communications between reporters and sources. The communications of the business officers of a news organization are *not* protected. A profession—journalism—is not a business.

Second, there is no doubt that "big" exposés sell newspapers, and it is likely that more stories of an exposé nature would appear under a privilege law. But exposés serve primarily to inform the public; that they may also increase sales is irrelevant. As the Supreme Court noted in *Time, Inc. v. Hill*: "That books, newspapers, and magazines are published and sold for profit does not prevent them from being a form of expression whose liberty is safeguarded by the First Amendment."[28]

Inherent in the argument that the privilege law would benefit a business enterprise is the assumption that the law will result in an increased flow of information to the public. That assumption is undoubtedly true. Thus, the benefit to the business enterprise will be the direct result of increasing the flow of information to American citizens. One can only weigh whether or not the "increased sales" *unnecessarily* benefit a business enterprise. And whatever the financial consequences, they are not the controlling factors in evaluating the advantages and disadvantages of a privilege law.

7. *A privilege law is not necessary because it would not affect the flow of news to the public.* Opponents of a privilege law often refer to the fact that the *New York Times* was considered one of the nation's best newspapers even before New York adopted a state privilege statute in 1970. The argument is, as the Supreme Court put it, that the press has "flourished" without having any privilege laws. Therefore, why is one necessary now?

The *New York Times* was undoubtedly a good newspaper and a comprehensive one prior to 1970. But that is not the issue. Privilege proponents do not argue that newspapers would not have items to print without access to confidential information. To the contrary, newspapers could print the facts contained in the hundreds of "handouts" and press releases they receive daily. The issue is whether or not newspapers miss out on news items in jurisdictions in which journalists do not have a privilege to withhold confidential information. The answer is, probably. "Probably," because such a statistic cannot be quantified. It is impossible to interview potential informants to ask them if the absence of a privilege is a determinant in their choice of whether or not to reveal the information they possess. There are no "hard data" to prove the impact of privilege legislation on the flow of news. But logic tells us that if a person has the slightest doubt about keeping his job or his health, it is extremely unlikely that he will jeopardize either by providing a reporter with the information in his possession if there is no legal protection for the communication. There is irony inherent in this primary argument against a privilege. And that logic is buttressed by evidence of the very real "chilling effect" on journalists and sources, as previously discussed.

The objections to a privilege law are not strong. The latter six discussed here are in fact rarely mentioned; those who oppose a privilege usually stick to the simple assertion that it would "harm the administration of justice," citing the prestigious Professor Wigmore as their principal source.

There is a *Catch-22* quality about the power to subpoena reporters to testify about confidential information and sources: regardless of the policies of the government in office, the retention of the power is essentially useless.

If the power to subpoena is utilized *infrequently*, it is difficult to argue that such power is "vital" to the effective administration of justice, since it is not used in the vast majority of cases. If it is utilized *frequently*, reporters quickly become "arms of the government" in the eyes of virtually all potential sources. Therefore, as the government continues to use the subpoena with increasing frequency, its power will ironically become less and less effective (assuming that there was some initial effectiveness). In a short time, subpoenaed information from reporters becomes useless even if the reporter is willing to talk, because all sources of confidential information will have "dried up." As Walter Cronkite put it: "Once it is established and believed that news correspondents are to be utilized in grand jury investigations, they will be of precious little value to such investigations because they will no longer have access to information that grand juries might want."[29]

PART IV

PROPOSED SOLUTIONS

10

Executive Guidelines, State Statutes and Proposed Federal Legislation

IF THE AMERICAN PUBLIC is to be fully informed, journalists must have legal protection for their sources and information. The courts have not provided that protection: the Supreme Court has determined that such protection is not a constitutional right. Thus, a legal privilege will have to come from the executive or legislative branches of government.

EXECUTIVE ACTION

The executive branch of government has generally been the adversary in the battle with the press. However, it has made at least one attempt to resolve or ameliorate the subpoena issue. In 1970, Attorney General John Mitchell released administration "guidelines" regarding the issuance of subpoenas to reporters.

In many respects, the guidelines were clearly concilia-tory. They conceded that "compulsory process in some cir-cumstances may have a limiting effect on the exercise of First Amendment rights."[1] They also established that all requests for subpoenas had to be authorized by the Attor-ney General himself.

Although the Justice Department's pronouncement ap-parently reduced tensions to some extent, the major issues of the controversy were not really resolved. The guidelines asserted that the government might subpoena unpublished information, even if confidential. And when "emergencies and other unusual situations" occur, the administration might issue a subpoena "which does not exactly conform to the guidelines."[2]

As H.R. Tatarian, vice-president of United Press Inter-national, observed after the rules were issued:

> The Justice Department's retreat may diffuse the debate but does not change the fact that the degree to which a newsman can honor a confidence depends solely on the courtesy, caprice, or political sensitivity of the prosecu-tor's office.[3]

STATE ACTION

Maryland was the first state to enact a statute. The Mary-land legislature passed a privilege law in 1896, which stood alone until the 1930s, when a series of privilege cases prompted other states to approve legislation. As of January 1973, nineteen states had adopted some type of privilege law, eight of them within the past decade. The states with privilege statutes and the dates they were enacted are:

1896—Maryland
1933—New Jersey
1935—Alabama
1936—Kentucky
1936—Arkansas
1937—Arizona
1937—Pennsylvania
1941—Ohio
1941—Indiana
1943—Montana

1949—Michigan
1964—Louisiana
1965—California
1967—New Mexico
1969—Nevada
1970—New York
1970—Alaska
1971—Rhode Island
1971—Illinois

Most of the state laws explicitly protect the identities of sources; only the Michigan, New York and Rhode Island laws specifically safeguard *information* communicated between the source and the newsman. The Pennsylvania statute has, however, been judicially interpreted to protect the communication as well as the source. In 1963 the *Philadelphia Bulletin* printed a series of articles on alleged graft in the city administration. The source for much of the data was the former Democratic ward leader and City Council sergeant at arms, John Fitzpatrick. A special grand jury summoned *Bulletin* president Robert Taylor and city editor Earl Selby to testify and bring tape recordings, memoranda, records of expenses incurred in gathering information from Fitzpatrick and "any and all other documents of or pertaining to John Fitzpatrick."[4] Both Taylor and Selby demurred and produced none of the requested materials, arguing that the 1937 Pennsylvania law protected them. Taylor said:

> Newspapers willing and courageous enough to fight for good government and against corruption regardless of forces or parties in power, as the *Bulletin* has done for many years, cannot provide their readers and the general public with important information unless their sources

are assured of protection as provided under the Act of 1937.[5]

The two journalists were initially fined a thousand dollars and sentenced to five-day prison terms for not complying. In an appeal to the Pennsylvania Supreme Court their conviction was overturned by a 6–1 margin. The court declared that the term "sources" referred to information as well as persons and argued forcefully for its interpretation of a broad privilege:

> . . . independent newspapers are today the principal watchdogs and protectors of honest, as well as good, government. They are, more than anyone else, the principal guardians of the general welfare of the community and, with few exceptions, they serve their city, State, or Nation with high principles, zeal, and fearlessness.
> . . . important information, tips and leads will dry up and the public will often be deprived of the knowledge of dereliction of public duty, bribery, corruption, conspiracy, and other crimes committed or possibly committed by public officials or powerful individuals or organizations, unless newsmen are able to fully and completely protect the sources of their information. It is vitally important that this public shield against governmental inefficiency, corruption, and crime be preserved against piercing and erosion.
> . . . the public welfare will be benefited more extensively and to a far greater degree by protection of all sources of disclosure of crime, conspiracy, and corruption than it would be by the occasional disclosure of the sources of newspaper information concerning a crime.[6]

However, no other state statute with the term "source" has been interpreted to mean information other than the name of the person who supplied confidential information. Most of the state statutes provide unqualified protection.

As Vince Blasi observed, "The aversion that most judges (and advocates) have for 'absolute' legal concepts seems not to have penetrated the walls of the state legislatures."[7]

Thirteen states have absolute privileges, and six states have some type of qualification.

In Alaska, if withholding a source's name would "result in a miscarriage of justice or the denial of a fair trial to those who challenge the privilege," or if it is deemed "contary to the public interest," the court can order the reporter to talk. The privilege is lost in Arkansas if a reporter writes articles "in bad faith, with malice, and not in the interest of the public welfare."

In Illinois a party seeking disclosure must demonstrate "the specific information sought and its relevancy to the proceedings; and a specific public interest which would be adversely affected if the factual information sought were not disclosed." The court also must determine that "all other available sources of information have been exhausted and disclosure of the information sought is essential to the protection of the public interest involved" before it can remove the privilege. Further, the privilege may not be invoked in a libel or slander action.

The protection does not hold in Louisiana if revealing the information is "essential to the public interest."

The standard for divesting the privilege in New Mexico is determined by a court if disclosure is "essential to prevent injustice," with the court considering "the nature of the proceeding, the merits of the claim or defense, the adequacy of the remedy otherwise available, the relevancy of the source, and the possibility of establishing by other means that which the source is offered as tending to prove."

The Rhode Island statute specifies that the privilege does not apply when a reporter asserts a defense based on his source of information as a defendant in a defamation suit, or to protect the source of any information required by law to be secret. The privilege may also be divested if there is "substantial evidence that disclosure of the information or of the source of information is necessary to permit a criminal prosecution for the commission of a specific felony, or to prevent a threat to human life, and that such information or the source of such information is not available from other prospective witnesses."

In fifteen of the states, the privilege may be invoked before any body with subpoena powers. However, in Illinois, Montana, Ohio and Rhode Island the statutory language does not explicitly indicate that the protection applies before state legislatures.

Most of the states provide coverage for any person "engaged in, connected with, or employed by" a newspaper or radio or television station. Several of the statutes, however, require that a reporter actually be paid to receive coverage. In New York the person must receive his "gain or livelihood" from journalism, and in Indiana he must receive his "principal income" as a reporter.

The types of publications persons must be "connected with" to receive coverage vary. All states include newspapers, and all but New Jersey and Michigan explicitly cover the broadcast media as well. Ten states cover "periodicals." Books are not explicitly mentioned in any of the statutes, but the Michigan law might be construed to cover such authors. Some of the states entitle only certain types of newspapers to protection. Indiana's law is the most stringent, requiring that the paper be issued at weekly intervals at least, that it conform to postal regulations, that it has been published in the same city or town for five consecutive years, and that it has a paid circulation of two percent of the population of the county in which it is published.

The recent series of cases involving reporters has spurred renewed activity in state legislatures. Although most state legislative sessions were only a few weeks old when this book went to press in early 1973, numerous bills to establish testimonial privileges for journalists had already been introduced in such states as Florida, Georgia, Hawaii, Kansas, Maine, Massachusetts, Mississippi, Missouri, Oregon, South Carolina, Tennessee, Texas, Washington and Wisconsin. States with shield statutes already on the books may amend and strengthen them: legislation to revise existing privilege laws has been introduced in Alaska, California, Maryland, New Mexico and Ohio.

FEDERAL ACTION

At the federal level, bills introduced in the House or the Senate have never been acted upon. Senator Arthur Capper (R–Kan.) introduced the first privilege legislation in Congress in 1929. Similar measures have been introduced periodically ever since. The following representatives and senators have sponsored legislation to establish a privilege:

71st Cong.	1929–1930	Sen. Arthur Capper (R–Kan.)
		Rep. Fiorello LaGuardia (R–N.Y.)
		Rep. Jacob Garber (R–Va.)
72d	1931–1932	Rep. LaGuardia
74th	1935–1936	Sen. Capper
		Rep. Edward Curley (D–N.Y.)
75th	1937–1938	Sen. Capper
		Rep. Curley
76th	1939–1940	Sen. Capper
		Rep. Curley
78th	1943–1944	Sen. Capper
82d	1951–1952	Rep. Louis Heller (D–N.Y.)
83rd	1953–1954	Rep. Frank Osmers (R–N.J.)
		Rep. Heller
84th	1955–1956	Rep. Osmers
86th	1959–1960	Rep. Francis Dorn (R–N.Y.)

		Rep. Donald Magnuson (D–Wash.)
		Rep. E. Ross Adair (R–Ind.)
		Sen. Kenneth Keating (R–N.Y.)
88th	1963–1964	Sen. Keating
		Rep. Sherman Lloyd (R–Utah)
		Rep. Seymour Halpern (R–N.Y.)
91st	1969–1970	Numerous sponsors
92d	1971–1972	Numerous sponsors of various bills
93rd Cong.	1973–1974	Numerous sponsors of various bills

Senator Ervin's Subcommittee on Constitutional Rights held hearings on this legislation and other free-press issues in late 1971 and early 1972. In the House, Representative Robert Kastenmeier (D–Wis.), chairman of House Judiciary Subcommittee No. 3, conducted hearings in September and October 1972. But no bill emanated from either subcommittee during the Ninety-second Congress.

In the Ninety-third Congress, both subcommittees held early hearings in February 1973. As this book went to press, neither committee had "reported out" a bill to be considered by the full judiciary committees and then by the House and Senate. The subcommittees were still considering the various types of legislation introduced.

PROPOSED LEGISLATION:
THE FREE FLOW OF INFORMATION ACT

Some individuals are concerned about the subpoenaing of journalists and its effects on the free flow of information and yet oppose legislative remedies as well. They argue that they prefer to rely on the protection of the First Amendment, noting that what Congress gives, Congress can take away.

Whatever merit that view once had vanished with the Supreme Court's decision in *Branzburg v. Hayes*. The court ruled that the First Amendment does *not* protect reporters from being compelled to testify. Thus, potential sources will hardly be convinced that their confidences will be maintained by the newsman "relying on the protection of the First Amendment." Pappas, Branzburg, Caldwell and scores of other reporters have "relied" on the First Amendment and have discovered that their reliance was misplaced.

It is true that Congress can repeal laws, and that constitutional provisions are more difficult to overturn. While one therefore might theoretically prefer a constitutional privilege to a legislative privilege, we no longer have the luxury of such a choice. The reality is that if Congress does not act, there will be no protection: reporters will continue to be subpoenaed, sources will continue to dry up, the flow of news will be further diminished.

In 1972 I made the following observations in an article in the *New York Times*:

> Study and debate will be required to fashion the best possible piece of legislation for this complex problem. The specifics of the legislation should be argued, but the need for some type of newsmen's privilege legislation should be obvious.[8]

During the past several years, my efforts have not been directed toward preaching the virtues of the particular legislation I have introduced. Rather, I have attempted to highlight the need for a federal shield law that offers broad coverage with few qualifications. As Vince Blasi observed in his study, "What really matters, in the judgment of many newsmen, is the basic recognition in principle of a newsman's privilege; the precise wording is not so important."[9]

Nevertheless, once a need for testimonial protection for journalists is recognized, legislation that effectively meets that need must be considered and drafted. A multitude of considerations must be analyzed in fashioning privilege legislation, many of which will be examined in this chapter.

But first, an initial question must be answered: Does Congress possess the power to determine forms of procedure, including whether or not there should be legislation enacted to create a privilege for journalists?

The answer is, In the federal system, yes. Congress clearly has such authority.

Although Congress is not empowered to interfere with the courts in their exercise of judicial power, it may establish forms of proceedings in the courts of the United States. The source of this authority is vested in Article III, Section One, of the U.S. Constitution, which authorizes Congress to establish inferior courts. The power of Congress to prescribe the forms of proceedings in U.S. courts was acknowledged as early as 1833 by the courts and has been recognized ever since. In 1833 a case concerning the establishment of federal courts in Louisiana was heard. In *Livingston v. Story* the Supreme Court declared:

> That Congress has the power to establish circuit and district courts, in any and all the states, and confer on them equitable jurisdiction, in cases coming within the Constitution, cannot admit of a doubt. It falls within the express words of the Constitution.
>
> "The judicial power of the United States shall be vested in one Supreme Court, and in such inferior courts as the Congress may, from time to time, ordain and establish."
>
> And the power to ordain and establish carries with it the power to prescribe and regulate the modes of proceedings in such courts, admits of as little doubt.[10]

And in *Ex parte The City Bank*, the Court declared: "Congress possesses the sole right to say what shall be the forms of proceedings, either in equity or in law, in the courts of the United States . . ."[11]

The power of Congress is not unlimited, however; Congress cannot enact unconstitutional rules of procedure, nor can it prescribe arbitrary or unreasonable rules. The Supreme Court, in *Tot v. U.S.*, stated:

> The rules of evidence, however, are established not alone by the courts but by the legislature. The Congress has power to prescribe what evidence is to be received in the Courts of the United States. The section under consideration is such legislation. But the due process clauses of the Fifth and Fourteenth Amendments set limits upon the power of Congress or that of a state legislature to make the proof of one fact or group of facts evidence of the existence of the ultimate fact upon which guilt is predicated.[12]

No court that has ruled on the validity of state privilege statutes has ever considered privilege statutes to be unconstitutional, arbitrary or unreasonable. The Free Flow of Information Act is clearly within the acceptable parameters of constitutional interpretation.

The existing rules in the courts of the United States in criminal cases are prescribed in Rule 26 of the Federal Rules of Criminal Procedure:

> In all trials the testimony of witness shall be taken orally in open court, unless otherwise provided by an Act of Congress or these rules. The admissibility of evidence and the competency and privileges of witnesses shall be governed, except when an Act of Congress or these rules otherwise provide by the principles of the common law as they may be interpreted by the courts of the United States in the light of reason and experience.[13]

Thus, in criminal cases before federal courts, the privileges of witnesses are determined by common-law rules, as interpreted by the courts. As already noted, there is no common-law basis for a journalists' privilege.

The rules in civil cases are determined by Rule 43(a) of the Federal Rules of Civil Procedure:

> In all trials the testimony of witnesses shall be taken orally in open court, unless otherwise provided by these rules. All evidence shall be admitted which is admissible under the statutes of the United States, or under the rules of evidence heretofore applied in the courts of the United States on the hearing of suits in equity, or under the rules of evidence applied in the courts of general jurisdiction of the State in which the United States court is held. In any case, the statute or rule which favors the reception of evidence governs and the evidence shall be presented according to the most convenient method prescribed in any of the statutes or rules to which reference is herein made. The competency of a witness to testify shall be determined in like manner.[14]

As both the Federal Rules of Criminal and Civil Procedure make clear, Congress possesses the authority to change rules of evidence or establish new rules of evidence for federal courts.

In the Supreme Court's decision in *Branzburg v. Hayes*, Justice White, speaking for the Court, acknowledged Congressional power to enact federal privilege legislation:

> At the federal level, Congress has freedom to determine whether a statutory newsman's privilege is necessary and desirable and to fashion standards and rules as narrow or broad as deemed necessary to address the evil discerned and, equally important, to re-fashion those rules as experience from time to time may dictate.[15]

Congress does *not* have the power to enact rules of evidence for state and local courts, however. Whether other legal theories could be employed to justify a Congressional act that covered state and local courts is open to question.

Former Assistant Attorney General Roger Cramton, in testimony before a House subcommittee, said:

> The only possible basis on which Congress could legislate to create a privilege in state proceedings would be the argument that since the First Amendment is incorporated in the 14th, Congress may do this in furtherance of its power under the 14th amendment to implement its provisions. If that allows it to implement the First Amendment, you could make an argument that Congress could legislate with respect to state proceedings. Whether or not that is so, it may be unwise as a matter of policy because it involves great issues of federalism.[16]

Joel Gora of the American Civil Liberties Union testified that, in his opinion, Congress could enact a statute that covered state as well as federal proceedings:

> If there is concern about the reach of Congressional power, I think the commerce clause provides an initial basis for writing a statute protective of the communication function, which Congress regulates in other fashions. I think these hearings can generate the kind of factfinding record . . . to support the conclusion that this kind of protection is necessary to effectuate the purposes of the first amendment.[17]

The question of Congressional power to establish a privilege in state courts involves complex legal problems. Since most recent cases have occurred in state proceedings, a uniform privilege applicable to state and federal courts clearly would be desirable. Although my bill covers only federal proceedings, I would support a bill that applied to state proceedings as well if it can be demonstrated that there is a constitutional basis for such Congressional action.

Once questions of Congressional power to establish a privilege are resolved, a number of other factors must be considered.

To which types of proceedings will the privilege apply? The legislation I have introduced specifies that the protection may be invoked before "the Congress or any Federal Court, grand jury, or administrative entity." The reporter is protected from subpoena by any body of the federal government.

Who is entitled to the protection? The Free Flow of Information Act covers any "person connected with or employed by the news media or press, or who is independently engaged in gathering information for publication or broadcast." This language is intentionally also extremely broad: freedom of the press is not a guarantee reserved only for those who work as television newscasters or reporters for large, metropolitan daily newspapers. This language covers those who work on college newspapers and for the "underground press" or weekly newspapers. It covers free-lance writers. And it would also cover an author such as David Halberstam in gathering information for such books as his *The Best and the Brightest*. In short, the bill covers all who work to publish or broadcast information citizens need to know about our government and our society. It seeks to ensure "the widest possible dissemination of information from diverse and antagonistic sources."[18]

One might argue that the terms of the statute are so broad that abuse is invited. For instance, might a bank robber refuse to testify about his robbery on the ground that he was planning to write a book on bank robberies and that therefore the whole area was privileged? Obviously, the answer is no (although he might invoke his Fifth Amendment privilege.) The courts, knowing the statutory as well as the general legislative intent, would be

ompetent, as they are in other areas of the law, to ferret
out abusive claims.

What is protected? The Free Flow of Information Act
protects from disclosure "any information or written, oral,
or pictorial material or the source of that information or
material procured for publication or broadcast."

Unlike most state statutes, the act protects *information*
itself as well as the source of information. In addition, the
language indicates that such materials as photographs and
tapes are covered. The only qualification is that the materials must be acquired in a person's capacity as a journalist
or news gatherer. For instance, if a reporter left work, went
home and witnessed a brawl in his own house, that information would not be privileged, because the information
was not "procured for publication or broadcast." In other
words, it is not a journalist per se who is covered—protection is afforded to a person only in his or her capacity as a
news gatherer.

However, the information does not have to be published
to be protected: as long as it is procured for publication
or broadcast it is covered. Otherwise, potential sources
would never know if their confidences were protected or
not, since protection would depend on the whim of the
editor who decides whether or not the story will be
published.

It should also be noted that there is no requirement that
the information protected be "confidential" information.
While the protection is aimed primarily at information
obtained in confidence, it is not limited to such information.
It could not be argued that a newspaper's photographs of
a demonstration are "confidential" information. Yet if the
government could subpoena such materials it could annex
press photographers as private investigative agents. The
act is designed to protect *all* information from the reach of
the subpoena. (Even if one wanted to protect only confi-

dential information, it would be virtually impossible to do
so, for the reporter himself would be the only arbiter of
whether or not the information was secured in confidence.)

Is the legislation absolute or qualified? This is one of the
most important—and difficult—questions to resolve in
formulating a privilege law. One must begin with the premise that the protection should be as absolute as possible if it
is to be effective in ensuring an independent press and in
providing a free flow of information to the public. Assuming that there are no competing interests, a totally absolute
law undoubtedly would be the most effective.

Some have argued that if an unqualified bill is not enacted, no legislation should be passed at all. While I do not
share that view, I do share the concern on which it is
premised. If legislation is not drafted to ensure that any
qualifications are both narrow and necessary, it will not
fulfill the purpose of ensuring a free flow of news to the
public. Ironically, if qualifications are too numerous or too
broad, the law, instead of protecting journalists, will sanction and thereby invite government subpoenas. Such a law
clearly *would* be worse than no law at all.

As I indicated in a speech in 1972 before the Associated
Press Managing Editors Association, "I do not relish the
idea of arguing against those who propose an absolute
privilege, for we are allies and not legislative opponents."[19]
Nevertheless, in my opinion, the Free Flow of Information
Act reasonably and realistically accounts for competing
interests without sacrificing the intended goal.

There is one specific instance in which protection would
not apply. If a reporter is a defendant in a libel case, and
he asserts a defense based upon the reliability of his source
of information, he may not invoke the privilege to refuse to
name his source and thereby preclude the court from exam-
ining the merits of his claim. In other words, the Free Flow
of Information Act cannot be utilized to emasculate existing libel laws.

It is likely that the courts would create such an exception if it were not explicitly included in the law. For example, although there are no exceptions in the New Jersey shield law concerning libel, the New Jersey Supreme Court has ruled that a "newspaper ought not to be able to give and take what it chooses when its own acts bring into question a liability on its part to others. If permitted to do as the defendant has here, the newspaper could give whatever information was favorable to its position and then plead the privilege to prevent any disclosure of the detrimental facts."[20]

Recent court decisions[21] indicate that the exception could not be used as a loophole to get reporters' sources and information, since the substance of the claim would have to be demonstrated before a journalist would be required to name his source in his own defense.

The libel exception is a narrow one. It does not detract from the total effect of the legislation, and it gives assurance to those who fear that the press could make libelous statements and then avoid all responsibility by hiding behind a privilege law.

In addition to the libel exception, the Free Flow of Information Act provides a means for divesting the privilege under unusual circumstances. A party seeking a reporter's information would have to apply to the U.S. District Court for an order divesting the privilege, and the application would be granted *only* if *all* of the following three conditions are satisfied by "clear and convincing evidence": (1) "there is probable cause to believe that the persons from whom the information is sought has information which is clearly relevant to a specific probable violation of the law; (2) the information sought cannot be obtained by alternative means; and (3) there is a compelling and overriding national interest in the information."

This was the standard suggested in the Branzburg case by the petitioning reporters, and this is the standard articulated by Justice Stewart in his dissenting opinion. If the Supreme Court vote had been 5–4 in the other direction, and the Court had ruled that there *is* a First Amendment right for reporters to withhold information, this standard would have applied.

Because the test for divestiture is so stringent, its use would be infrequent. However, occasions might arise when such a procedure would be necessary, as was pointed out in one of the amicus curiae briefs for the reporters in the Branzburg cases:

> The suggested standard recognizes that there may be occasions on which human life—or the life of the community or nation—may be so clearly at stake that no reasonable person should expect newsmen, lawyers, physicians or anyone else in a confidential relationship to withhold such information—for example, information about a murder plot or plans for violent civil insurrection. Indeed, if such a test were adopted by the Court, it is not likely that courts would often find the need to compel newsmen's testimony on these matters.[22]

The Supreme Court has always held that intrusion into First Amendment areas can only be permitted in those instances where there is a "compelling and overriding governmental interest."[23] Although the Court determined that reporters' information is *not* protected by the First Amendment, it is my view that First Amendment values indeed are involved. It is the people's right to know that is at stake, and that is why I believe that if the law is to be qualified, a test less stringent than this traditional First Amendment standard should not be adopted.

PART V
CONCLUSION

11

A Time
to Act

IT IS NOTEWORTHY that proponents and opponents
of a journalists' privilege cannot be categorized according
to party or ideological patterns. Republicans and Demo-
crats, "conservatives" and "liberals"—the supporters have
only one common identity, and that is a desire to ensure
strong, independent news media for the nation.

A free and unencumbered press is an absolute prerequi-
site for American survival and progress during the final
decades of the twentieth century. Pennsylvania Judge
Musmanno eloquently emphasized the importance of all
the elements required for a truly free press:

> Freedom of the press is not restricted to the operation
> of linotype machines and printing presses. A rotary press

needs raw material like a flour mill needs wheat. A print shop without material to print would be as meaningless as a vineyard without grapes, an orchard without trees, or a lawn without verdure.

Freedom of the press means freedom to gather news, write it, publish it, and circulate it. When any one of these integral operations in interdicted, freedom of the press becomes a river without water.[1]

The enactment of the Free Flow of Information bill or similar legislation will guarantee that the integral operation of gathering the news will not be interdicted.

My hope is that this book will stimulate and contribute to public debate and discussion of this issue. In the final analysis, as Alexander Hamilton observed, the security of freedom of the press, "whatever fine declarations may be inserted in any constitution respecting it, must altogether depend upon public opinion, and on the general spirit of the people and of the government."[2]

This observation has not lost its validity during the past two hundred years. The *Chicago Tribune* echoed Hamilton's remarks in 1973:

The sad thing about the recent drift away from press freedom is that it has come about not because of Communist conquest, not mainly because of totalitarian decrees, not even as the result of conscious public policy— but rather through a gradual process of osmosis—as in the United States—which could not proceed were it not for the apathy of the public and, in some instances, even the press.[3]

If the "gradual process of osmosis" is not halted soon, the great American experiment in democracy will be.

CHAPTER NOTES

Chapter 1

1. "Free Press Imperiled, Group Says," *Wash. Post*, Jan. 1, 1973, A24.
2. *Id.*
3. "The Fading Ring of Freedom," *Chicago Tribune*, Jan. 5, 1973, 12.
4. *Supra*, note 1.
5. Fred Powledge, *ACLU* Reports, "The Nixon Administration and the Press: The Engineering of Restraint," Sept. 1971, 5.
6. *Id.*, 13.
7. *Hearings Before the Subcommittee on Constitutional Rights of the Committee on the Judiciary*, U.S. Senate, 92d Cong., 1st and 2d Sess., 1971 and 1972, Statement of Nicholas Johnson, 793. [The Hearings are hereinafter referred to as "*Senate Hearings*."]
8. *Supra*, note 5, at 17.
9. "Dr. Whitehead and the First Amendment," *Wash. Post*, Dec. 22, 1972, A22.
10. *Id.*
11. Alan Kriegsman, "An Era of Timidity on TV?" *Wash. Post*, Jan. 21, 1973, F9.
12. "FOP Cites Abuse in Print, Looks to Nixon for Curbs," *Cleveland Plain Dealer*, Jan. 12, 1973, 11C.
13. *Senate Hearings*, Statement of Senator Ervin, 1.
14. See *The Federalist*, No. 84, 514 (Rossiter, ed. 1961).
15. See E. Dumbauld, *The Bill of Rights* 33 (1957).
16. U.S. Constitution, 1st Amend.
17. *The Papers of Thomas Jefferson*, Vol. XI, 49 (1955).
18. *In re Mack*, 386 Pa. 251, 126 A.2d 679 (1956).
19. *Senate Hearings*, Statement of Senator Ervin, 4.
20. Journalist's Code of Ethics, adopted by the Newspaper Guild, First Annual Convention, 1934.
21. Freedom of the Press Act of April 15, 1949, esp. Art. 4, Chap. 3.

22. Oikendenkaymiskaari, Chap. 17, Art. XXIV.

23. See e.g., Baden-Württemberg-Landespressegesetz—1952 (Bundesgesetzbl. I.S. 177) §66 Abs. 2 des Gesetzes über Ordnungswidrigkeiten.

24. Federal Law of Austria, 1922, para. 45; Civil Law Stat. of Austria, Code V, Art. 321.

25. *Branzburg v. Hayes*, 408 U.S. 665, 32 L.Ed. 2d 626 (1972).

Chapter 2

1. "Piracies of the Washington Lobby—The Land Robbers," *N.Y. Times,* Jan. 6, 1857, 4.

2. *Congressional Globe*, 34th Cong., 3rd Sess. (1857), 275.

3. *Id.*, 403.

4. *Id.*

5. *Senate Miscellaneous Document No. 278*, 53rd Cong., 2d Sess., 1894, 103. [Hereinafter referred to as *Senate Doc. 278*.]

6. *Id.*, 105.

7. *Id.*, 115.

8. *Id.*, 108.

9. *Supra*, note 2, at 411.

10. *Senate Doc. 278*, 191.

11. *Id.*, 509.

12. *Id.*, 331.

13. *Id.*, 316.

14. *N.Y. Tribune*, May 16, 1871.

15. *Senate Doc. 278*, 325.

16. *Supra*, note 14.

17. *Senate Doc. 278*, 856.

18. *Ex Parte Lawrence*, 116 Cal. 298, 300, 48 P. 124 (1897).

19. "Editor, Mum on Letter Writer's Identity, Fined $25 by Kentucky House," *Editor and Publisher*, Mar. 17, 1934, 5,6.

20. Steigleman, "Newspaper Confidence Laws," *Journalism Quarterly*, Sept. 1943, 236.

21. "Senators Stop Quiz into Reporter's Source," *Editor and Publisher*, May 10, 1952, 8.

22. *Id.*

23. See *N.Y. Times*, April 10, 1963, 22.

24. "Reporter Refuses to Tell Senate Who Gave Him Data on TFX," *N.Y. Times*, May 25, 1963, 6.

25. Although I would have preferred a "straight" vote on the contempt motion, I voted to recommit the motion to committee, thus effectively killing the contempt move.

26. Harlan Draeger, "Jailed Reporter No Hero—Just Convinced American Freedom of Press Not Personal, But Public, Prerogative," *The Oregonian*, Jan. 8, 1973.

27. *Hearings Before Subcommittee No. 3, House Judiciary Committee, House of Representatives*, 92d Cong., 2d Sess., 1972, Statement of Rep. Dan Kuykendall, 195. [Hereinafter referred to as *House Hearings*.]

28. *Supra*, note. 26.

29. "Legal Opinion May Ease Path for Newsman Facing Charge," *Memphis Commercial Appeal*, Dec. 7, 1972, 9.

30. "U.S. Investigating Charges of 'Leak' on Soybean Crop," *N.Y. Times*, May 27, 1966, 30.

31. "Columnist Fights FTC Subpoena for His Notes," *N.Y. Times*, Sept. 2, 1971, 12.

32. "FTC Subpoena of Writer Voided," *N.Y. Times*, Sept. 28, 1971, 17.

Chapter 3

1. *Burdick v. United States*, 236 U.S. 79 (1915); *Curtin v. United States*, 236 U.S. 96 (1915).

2. "Court Drops Sloan Contempt Charge," *Editor and Publisher*, Aug. 11, 1934, 10.

3. *Id.*

4. "Upholds Press Confidences," *Editor and Publisher*, Aug. 24, 1935, 6.

5. *State of New York Law Revision Commission, Leg. Doc. No. 65(A)*, 1949, 64.

6. *Rosenberg v. Carroll, In re Lyons*, 99 F.Supp. 629 (1951).

7. *Thompson v. State*, 284 Minn. 274, 275, 170 N.W.2d 101 (1969).

8. *Id.*, 278.

9. "Newsmen Subpoena Refused by Judge," *Wash. Post*, April 8, 1970.

10. "Judge Denies Move for Reporter's Notes," *Wash. Post*, April 8, 1970.

11. "Foard Attacks News Articles," *Columbia State*, Aug. 15, 1972, B1.
12. *Id.*
13. "Two Reporters Prefer Jail," *Wash. Star*, Dec. 16, 1972, A5.
14. "Tapes Demanded by Jury," *N.Y. Times*, Dec. 21, 1972, 23.
15. Telephone conversation with Art Schreiber, Jan. 22, 1973.
16. *In re Wayne*, 4 Hawaii Dist. Ct. 475, 476 (1914).
17. "Newsman Yields on Source," *N.Y. Times*, July 28, 1961, 44.
18. "Two Newsmen Freed in Contempt Case," *N.Y. Times*, Mar. 31, 1967, 24.

Chapter 4

1. *Pledger v. State*, 77 Ga. 242, 245, 2 S.E. 320, 1886.
2. *Id.*, 248.
3. *Brogan v. Passaic Daily News*, 22 N.J. 139, 152, 123 A.2d 473, 480 (1956).
4. *Beecroft v. Point Pleasant Printing and Publishing Co.*, 197 A.2d 416 (1964).
5. *Garland v. Torre*, 259 F.2d 545 (2d Cir.), *cert. denied*, 358 U.S. 910 (1958).
6. *Application of Cepeda*, 233 F.Supp. 465 (1964).
7. *Id.*
8. *New York Times Co. v. Sullivan*, 376 U.S. 254 at 279, 280 (1964).
9. *Cervantes v. Time, Inc.*, 330 F.Supp. 936, 940 (1970).
10. *Cervantes v. Time, Inc.*, 464 F.2d 986, 993 (1972).
11. Brit Hume, "A Chilling Effect on the Press," *N.Y. Times Mag.*, Dec. 17, 1972, 13.
12. "Seattle Reporter Is Ordered Jailed," *N.Y. Times*, May 20, 1939, 10.
13. "High Court Rejects a Newsman's Petition for Review," *N.Y. Times*, Nov. 14, 1972.
14. Petition for a Writ of Certiorari, *Farr v. Superior Court of Los Angeles County*, U.S. Supreme Court, October Term 1971, No. 71-1642, 168, 169.
15. *Id.*, 171.
16. *Id.*, 217.

17. *Id.*, 218.
18. "Newsman on Coast Sent to Jail Until He Reveals Source of Data," *N.Y. Times*, Nov. 17, 1972, 24.
19. "New Steps Taken to Release Farr, Branded 'Martyr,' " *Editor and Publisher*, Dec. 2, 1972, 10.
20. "Who's Hobbling the Press?" *New Republic*, Dec. 16, 1972, 6.
21. "Imprisoned Press," *N.Y. Times*, Nov. 17, 1972, 44.
22. *Id.*
23. *People v. Durrant*, 116 Cal. 179, 220, 48 P. 75 (1897).
24. *Plunkett v. Hamilton*, 136 Ga. 72, 81, 70 S.E. 781 (1911).
25. *Id.*, 84.
26. *In re Grunow*, 84 N.J.L. 235, 236, 85 A. 1011 (1913).
27. *Id.*
28. "Three Reporters Are Sent to Jail in Contempt Case," *Wash. Star*, Oct. 30, 1929, 2.
29. "Virginia Editor Jailed for Contempt," *Editor and Publisher*, Jan. 9, 1932, 7.
30. *Id.*
31. *Id.*
32. *Id.*
33. "Chicago Court Defers Contempt Ruling," *Editor and Publisher*, Aug. 4, 1934, 3.
34. "Reporters Victors in Contempt Case," *N.Y. Times*, Aug. 4, 1934, 13.
35. *Supra*, note 33.
36. *Id.*, 4.
37. *Id.*
38. *State of New York Law Revision Commission, Leg. Doc. No. 65(A)*, 1949, 19.
39. *Id.*, 22.
40. *People ex. rel. Mooney v. Sheriff of New York County*, 269 N.Y. 291, 199 N.E. 415, 416 (1936).
41. "Guilty of Concealing News Sources," *N.Y. Times*, Sept. 13, 1939.
42. "Jailed Newsmen Plead for Confidence Law," *Editor and Publisher*, Mar. 6, 1948, 7.
43. *Id.*
44. *Id.*, 8.
45. *Murphy v. Colorado* (Colo. Sup. Ct., unreported opinion), *cert. denied*, 365 U.S. 843 (1961).
46. "Reporter Ends Jail Term," *N.Y. Times*, May 4, 1961, 40.

47. *In re Goodfader's Appeal*, 45 Hawaii 317, 319, 367 P.2d 472 (1961).
48. *Id.*
49. *Id.*, 329.
50. *Id.*, 327.
51. *Id.*, 333.
52. *State v. Buchanan*, 436 P.2d 729, 730 (1967).
53. *Id.*, 732.
54. *State v. Buchanan*, 250 Ore. 244, 436 P.2d 729, *cert. denied*, 392 U.S. 905 (1968).
55. *State v. Knops*, 183 N.W.2d 93 (Sup. Ct. Wisc. 1971).
56. *Id.*

Chapter 5

1. Brief for Petitioner, *In re Pappas*, U.S. Supreme Court, October Term, 1971, No. 70-94, 9.
2. *Id.*, 10.
3. *In re Pappas*, 266 N.E.2d 297 (Mass., 1971).
4. Petition for a Writ of Certiorari, *In re Pappas*, U.S. Supreme Court, October Term, 1970, No. 70-94, 12a.
5. *Supra*, note 1, at 10.
6. *Id.*, 43.
7. *Id.*
8. *Id.*, 45.
9. *Id.*, 46.
10. Petition for Certiorari, *Branzburg v. Hayes*, U.S. Supreme Court, October Term 1970, No. 70-85, 67.
11. Kentucky Revised Statutes, 421.100.
12. *Supra*, note 10.
13. *Id.*, 26.
14. *Id.*, 33.
15. *Id.*
16. *Id.*
17. *Id.*, 36, 37.
18. *Id.*, 33.
19. Petition for Certiorari, *United States v. Caldwell*, U.S. Supreme Court, October Term 1970, No. 70–57, Appendix 17.
20. Earl Caldwell, "Ask Me. I Know. I Was the Test Case," *Saturday Review*, Aug. 5, 1972, 4, 5.

21. *Supra*, note 19.
22. *Id.*
23. *Supra*, note 2.
24. *Supra*, note 19.
25. Brief for Respondent, *United States v. Caldwell*, U.S. Supreme Court, October Term 1971, No. 70-57, 7.
26. *Id.*, 9.
27. *Caldwell v. United States*, 434 F.2d 1081, 1086 (1970).
28. *Id.*, 1090.
29. *Id.*, 1092.
30. *Id.*
31. *Supra*, note 25, at 43, 44.
32. See Chapter 9, notes 21 and 22, and accompanying text.
33. See Antell, *The Modern Grand Jury: Benighted Super Government* 51 A.B.A.J. 153 (1965). See also Donner and Cerruti, *The Grand Jury Network: How the Nixon Administration Has Secretly Perverted a Traditional Safeguard of Individual Rights*, 214 *The Nation* 5 (1972).
34. See 35 Nebraska L. Rev. 562, n.4 (1956).
35. *Supra*, note 20.

Chapter 6

1. "Is Radio on the Record?" *N.Y. Times*, Mar. 5, 1972, IV, 3.
2. "Hogan Answers Appeal by WBAI," *N.Y. Times*, April 30, 1972, 112.
3. "Goodman and WBAI Freed of Contempt," *N.Y. Times*, June 14, 1972, 95.
4. Petition for a Writ of Certiorari, *Bridge v. New Jersey*, U.S. Supreme Court, October Term, 1972, No. 72-923, 55a-57a.
5. N.J.S.A. 2A:84A-21.
6. *Supra*, note 4, at 5a.
7. *Id.*, 54a.
8. *Id.*, 8.
9. *Lightman v. State*, 15 Md. App. 713, at 714-715 (1972).
10. Md. Code, Art. 35, §2.
11. *Supra*, note 9, at 724.
12. *Id.*
13. *Id.*, 725.
14. *Id.*, 726.

15. Brief for Respondent-Appellants, *New York v. Dan* and *Barnes*, N.Y. Supreme Court, Appellate Division, Fourth Dept., 5,6.
16. *Id.*, 7.
17. Appellant-Petitioner's Brief in the Supreme Court of the State of Delaware, No. 209, Dec. 22, 1972, 5. (Petition of Charles McGowan.)
18. "TV Host Defies Jury, Refuses to Name Caller," *Wash. Star*, Nov. 29, 1972, A2.
19. *Id.*
20. *House Hearings*, 246.
21. *Id.*
22. William Thomas, "Warts and All, Our Cause Is Your Cause," *Los Angeles Times*, Dec. 24, 1972, C-1.

Chapter 7

1. George Seldes (ed.), *The Great Quotations*, 1966.
2. H. L. Mencken, *A New Dictionary of Quotations on Historical Principles*, 1946.
3. American Newspapers Publishers Association Foundation, *Speaking of a Free Press*, Feb. 1970.
4. *Thomas v. Collins*, 323 U.S. 516, 530 (1945).
5. *Grosjean v. American Press Co.*, 297 U.S. 233, 249 (1936).
6. *Associated Press v. U.S.*, 326 U.S. 1, 20 (1945).
7. Curtis MacDougall, *The Press and Its Problems*, 1964, 321.
8. *Id.*, 320.
9. Petition for a Writ of Certiorari, *United States v. Caldwell*, U.S. Supreme Court, October Term 1970, No. 70-57, Appendix 52-53. [Hereinafter, Petition for Certiorari, *Caldwell*.]
10. *Id.*, 59, 60.
11. Letter from A.M. Rosenthal, July 29, 1971.
12. Letter from Charles Whipple, Aug. 3, 1971.
13. Letter from Reg Murphy, Aug. 2, 1971.
14. Letter from Clayton Kirkpatrick, Aug. 16, 1971.
15. Letter from James Bucknam, July 29, 1971.
16. *Supra*, note 9.
17. *Id.*, 55.
18. Letter from Arthur Bertelson, July 28, 1971.

19. *Id.*
20. Letter from John McMullan, July 29, 1971.
21. *Id.*
22. *Supra*, note 14.
23. *Supra*, note 13.
24. *Supra*, note 12.
25. *Id.*
26. Letter from William Niese, Sept. 1, 1971.
27. *Id.*
28. *House Hearings*, 219.
29. *Supra*, note 20.
30. Deposition of Max Frankel, *Caldwell v. United States*, U.S. District Court.
31. *Id.*
32. *Supra*, note 18.
33. *Supra*, note 17.
34. Vince Blasi, *Press Subpoenas: An Empirical and Legal Analysis*, 1971, 20, 21.
35. *Supra*, note 9, at 46, 47.
36. Brit Hume, "A Chilling Effect on the Press, *N.Y. Times Mag.*, Dec. 17, 1972, 89.
37. William Thomas, "Warts and All, Our Cause Is Your Cause," *Los Angeles Times*, Dec. 24, 1972, C-1.
38. *Id.*
39. *Id.*
40. "Writs Against Reporters Arouse Debate," *N.Y. Times*, Jan. 7, 1973, 1, 60.
41. *Supra*, note 36, at 78.
42. *House Hearings*, 239.
43. *Id.*
44. "Writer on Alioto Is Silent on Sources," *N.Y. Times*, April 29, 1970, 35.
45. *Supra*, note 18.
46. *NAACP v. Button*, 371 U.S. 415, 433 (1963).
47. "News Techniques Stressed in Trial," *N.Y. Times*, April 5, 1970, 28.
48. *Id.*
49. *Supra*, note 40.
50. *House Hearings*, 211.
51. *Supra*, note 9, at 44, 45.
52. *Supra*, note 34, at 50.

Chapter 8

1. "Subpoenas on the Press," *N.Y. Times*, Feb. 4, 1970, 42.
2. William Thomas, "Warts and All, Our Cause Is Your Cause," *Los Angeles Times*, Dec. 24, 1972, C-1.
3. Fred Powledge, *ACLU Reports*, 45.
4. "The Subpoena Dilemma," *Columbia Journalism Review*, Spring 1970, 3.
5. James McCartney, "Must the Media Be 'Used'?" *Columbia Journalism Review*, Winter 1969-1970, 36.
6. *House Hearings*, 237. [Citing attorney Floyd Abrams in the March/April issue of *Trial* magazine, 1972.]
7. James Doyle, "Official Access—A Threat to Press Freedom," *Providence Journal*, Feb. 5, 1970.
8. *Supra*, note 3, at A-2.
9. Vince Blasi, *Press Subpoenas*, 147.
10. *Branzburg v. Hayes*, 408 U.S. 665 (1972).
11. *Id.*
12. Lawrence Velvel, *The Supreme Court Stops the Presses*, unpublished paper, 1972.
13. *Supra*, note 10.
14. 362 U.S. 60, 1960.
15. *Id.*, 64, 65.
16. 372 U.S. 539, 1963.

Chapter 9

1. See 8 J. Wigmore, *Evidence* (McNaughton, rev. 1961), 2192.
2. *Id.*, 2285.
3. J. A. Guest and A. L. Stanzler, "The Constitutional Argument for Newsman Concealing Their Sources," 64 N.W. L. Rev. 18, 27 (1969).
4. Abraham Goldstein, "Newsmen and Their Confidential Sources," *New Republic*, Mar. 21, 1970, 14.
5. Petition for a Writ of Certiorari, *United States v. Caldwell*, U.S. Supreme Court, October Term 1970, No. 70-57, Appendix 32. [Affidavit of Anthony Ripley.]
6. *Id.*
7. *Id.*

8. Julian Goodman, address before the Sigma Delta Chi Foundation, University of Texas, Austin, Texas, Mar. 10, 1970.

9. One indication of "community support" is the correlation between publicized cases and the subsequent enactment of a shield law. The first state statute, in Maryland in 1896, was in response to a publicized subpoena case. Many other state laws have similar origins. Recently, the California legislature changed its state statute in response to the William Farr case, and the New Jersey legislature passed the "Peter Bridge" bill in December, in response to Bridge's plight.

10. The Gallup findings were based on in-person interviews with 1,462 adults 18 and older in more than 300 localities across the country between November 10 and November 13, 1972. The following question was asked: "Suppose a newspaper reporter obtains information for a news article he is writing from a person who asks that his name be withheld. Do you think that the reporter should or should not be required to reveal the name of this man if he is taken to court to testify about the information in his news article?" The findings were that 57% said the reporter "should not be required" to reveal his sources; 34% said the reporter "should be required" to do so; and 9% had no opinion. There was little difference in terms of age, sex, race, and politics of the respondents, but there were sharp differences according to educational background:

	Should Not	Should	No Opinion
College Background	68	27	5
High School Background	55	37	8
Grade School Background	48	35	17

See "57% Don't Want Newsmen to Name Their Sources," *Editor and Publisher*, Dec. 9, 1972, 13.

11. *VI Writings of James Madison 1790-1802*, 387 (cited in *In re Goodfader*, 45 Hawaii 317, 352).

12. Vince Blasi, *Press Subpoenas: An Empirical and Legal Analysis*, 68.

13. "The Subpoena Dilemma," *Columbia Journalism Review*, Spring 1970, 3.

14. Letter from John McMullan, July 29, 1971.

15. *Supra*, note 1, at 2374.

16. *Id.*

17. *Rovario v. U.S.* 353 U.S. 53, 59 (1957).
18. John Hohenberg, *The News Media: A Journalist Looks at His Profession*, 1968, 260.
19. *Supra*, note. 14.
20. 14 Albany L. Rev. 16 (1950).
21. Although Herbert Ahlswede, Chief Deputy of the Criminal Division of the Nevada Attorney General's Office, reports that "we have had no problems directly concerned with the newsmen's privilege law," he went on to say, "I am personally opposed to this newsman's privilege law because of its potential interference with law enforcement and the potential abuses which could arise from the claim of privilege." (Letter from Herbert Ahlswede, Oct. 27, 1972.) Arizona Attorney General Gary Nelson believes that the Arizona statute "does have a debilitating effect on our office's efforts at law enforcement." (Letter from Gary Nelson, Oct. 11, 1972.)
22. Arkansas Attorney General Ray Thornton's Office reports that "our office has not encountered any difficulties from this statute" (letter of Oct. 11, 1972); California Attorney General Evelle Younger said California shield statute provisions "have not significantly hampered California's efforts to prosecute for criminal violations" (letter of Oct. 25, 1972); Maryland Attorney General Francis Burch states that "the Maryland experience has been that such a limited privilege has not seriously impeded its law enforcement efforts" (letter of Oct. 24, 1972); Montana Attorney General Robert Woodahl said that "no incidents have arisen where information collected by a newsman has come into conflict with the requirements of law enforcement" (letter of Nov. 1, 1972); and New Mexico Assistant Attorney General Ronald Van Amberg notes that the statute "has not interfered with our prosecution of criminal cases" (letter of Nov. 14, 1972).
23. Letter from William Brown, Oct. 24, 1972.
24. Letter from John Havelock, Nov. 9, 1972.
25. Letter from Frank Kelley, Oct. 18, 1972.
26. "Writs Against Reporters Arouse Debate," *N.Y. Times*, Jan. 7, 1973, 1, 60.
27. 11 Ark. L. Rev. 117, 126 (1957).
28. 385 U.S. 374, 397 (1967).
29. *Supra*, note 5, at 52-53. [Affidavit of Walter Cronkite.]

Chapter 10

1. Attorney General's Guidelines, 39 U.S.L.W. 2111 (Aug. 25, 1970).
2. *Id.*
3. "Mitchell Assures Newsmen on Files," *N.Y. Times*, Feb. 6, 1970, 40.
4. *In re Taylor*, 193 A.2d 181 (1963).
5. "Philadelphia Bulletin Fights to Shield Its News Sources," *Editor and Publisher*, Jan. 26, 1963, 9.
6. "Newsmen Upheld on Secret Source," *N.Y. Times*, July 16, 1963, 17.
7. Vince Blasi, *Press Subpoenas: An Empirical and Legal Analysis*, 95.
8. Charles Whalen, Jr., "Should Newsmen Keep Secrets," *N.Y. Times*, July 24, 1972, 27.
9. *Supra*, note 7, at 68.
10. 9 Pet. 632, 655 (1833).
11. 3 How. 292, 317 (1845).
12. 319 U.S. 467, 473 (1943).
13. *Federal Rules of Criminal Procedure*, 18 U.S.C., Rule 26.
14. *Federal Rules of Civil Procedure*, 28 U.S.C., Rule 43(a).
15. *Branzburg v. Hayes*, 408 U.S. 665 (1972).
16. *House Hearings*, 41.
17. *Id.*, 231.
18. *Associated Press v. U.S.* 326 U.S. 1, 20 (1945).
19. Speech of Charles W. Whalen, Jr., before the Associated Press Managing Editors Association, Kansas City, Missouri, Nov. 16, 1972.
20. *Brogan v. Passaic Daily News*, 22 N.J. 139, 123 A.2d 473 (1956).
21. See e.g., *Cervantes v. Time, Inc.*, 464 F.2d 986 (1972).
22. Brief for Radio Television News Directors Association, as Amicus Curiae, U.S. Supreme Court, *United States v. Caldwell*, No. 70–57, 10, 11.
23. See e.g., *Gibson v. Florida Legislative Investigation Committee*, 372 U.S. 539, 547 (1963).

Chapter 11

1. *In re Mack*, 386 Pa. 251, 126 A.2d 679 (1956).
2. See *The Federalist*, No. 84, 514 (Rossiter, ed. 1961).
3. "The Fading Ring of Freedom," *Chicago Tribune*, Jan. 5, 1973, 12.

SELECTED BIBLIOGRAPHY

BLASI, Vince, *Press Subpoenas: An Empirical and Legal Analysis*, A Study Report for the Reporters' Committee for Freedom of the Press, 1971.

CHAFEE, Zechariah, *Freedom of Speech*, New York, Harcourt, Brace, 1920.

Freedom of the Press, Hearings Before the Subcommittee on Constitutional Rights of the Committee on the Judiciary, U.S. Senate, 92d Cong., 1st and 2d Sess., 1971 and 1972.

HAIMAN, Franklyn, *Freedom of Speech—Issues and Cases*, New York, Random House, 1965.

HOHENBERG, John, *The News Media: A Journalist Looks at His Profession*, New York, Holt, Rinehart & Winston, 1968.

JOHNSON, Nicholas, *How to Talk Back to Your Television Set*, New York, Bantam, 1970.

LEVY, Leonard, *Legacy of Suppression*, New York, Harper & Row, 1963.

MACDOUGALL, Curtis, *The Press and Its Problems*, Dubuque, Iowa, Brown, 1964.

The Newsman's Privilege, Committee Print, Committee on the Judiciary, U.S. Senate, 89th Cong., 2d Sess., 1966.

Newsman's Privilege, Hearings Before Subcommittee No. 3, House Judiciary Committee, House of Representatives, 92d Cong., 2d Sess., 1972.

POWLEDGE, Fred, *ACLU Reports: The Nixon Administration and the Engineering of Restraint*, 1971.

Press Freedom Under Pressure, Twentieth Century Task Force, Nov. 1971.

SMALL, William, *Political Power and the Press*, New York, Norton, 1972.

State of New York Law Revision Commission, Leg. Doc. No. 65(A), 1949.

ZINN, Howard, *Disobedience and Democracy*, New York, Vintage, 1968.

About The Author

Congressman CHARLES W. WHALEN, JR., a Republican, is serving his fourth term as a member of the United States House of Representatives. He is a member of the House Foreign Affairs Committee and two of its subcommittees—the Foreign Economic Policy Subcommittee and the Inter-American Affairs Subcommittee. Prior to his election to Congress, Mr. Whalen was professor of economics at the University of Dayton and chairman of the Department of Economics.

A graduate of the University of Dayton, Congressman Whalen received a master's degree from the Harvard University Graduate School of Business Administration in 1946. He has taken doctoral work in economics at the Ohio State University and received an honorary doctor of laws degree from Central State University (Ohio) in 1966.

A veteran of World War II, Congressman Whalen is married to the former Barbara Gleason and is the father of four sons and two daughters. He and four other Congressmen co-authored a book, *How to End the Draft: The Case for an All-Volunteer Army*, published in 1967 by The National Press Inc., Washington, D.C.

VINTAGE HISTORY—AMERICAN